SUPER GOOD

BAKING FOR KIDS

THIS BOOK
IS FOR
MY MUFFIN.
I GOT THE
BEST ONE.

DUFF GOLDMAN
SUPER GOOD
BAKING FOR KIDS

HARPER
An Imprint of HarperCollinsPublishers

CONTENTS

INTRODUCTION:
MISE EN PLACE
7

CHAPTER 1
COOKIES
27

CHAPTER 2
PÂTE À CHOUX
43

CHAPTER 3
DONUTS
61

CHAPTER 4
BEAR CLAWS,
MONKEY BREAD, SWEET STREET
TACOS, & MORE
77

CHAPTER 5
CUPCAKES
105

CHAPTER 6
CAKES
123

CHAPTER 7
PIES
153

CHAPTER 8
BROWNIES & BARS
175

CHAPTER 9
TARTS
187

Glossary 202
Measurement Conversions 204
Index 205

ENTS

INTRODUCTION:

· MISE EN PLACE ·

Mise en place is French for "things in place." When we cook, we always have more fun and make better stuff when we set up. We make sure we have all of our ingredients, we make sure we have all of our tools, and we make sure that the kitchen is clean. When I bake, I have a routine: I always start by cleaning the kitchen. Then I read the recipe and get out anything that needs to be brought to room temperature, like butter or eggs (see Kitchen Basics). I also assemble all the equipment I need, and all the flour, sugar, chocolate, and any other ingredients I need for the recipe I'm doing. And now I'm ready to bake. Just like there is mise en place for baking, there's also mise en place for this book. I'm not only gonna show you how to bake, I'm gonna show you how to *get ready* to bake!

KITCHEN SAFETY ·

ALL RECIPES SHOULD BE DONE UNDER ADULT SUPERVISION

Being safe is the first step to having fun in the kitchen and making delicious things.

KEEP THE KITCHEN CLEAN: The kitchen is my favorite room in the house, so I keep it really, really clean! A clean kitchen is a safe kitchen.

PUT EVERYTHING BACK WHERE IT BELONGS: I make sure all of my tools are properly put away, so I always know where they are when I need them.

KNOW WHAT IS DANGEROUS: There's lots of sharp and dangerous things in the kitchen, so I make sure that I'm very organized and I know where all of those sharp things are, and I know what's dangerous. Go through your kitchen with an adult and make sure they show what you are allowed to touch and what you're not.

ALWAYS WASH KNIVES BY HAND: Never put knives in the dishwasher. This makes the blades dull, and when a knife is dull it is easier to cut yourself. Also, someone might reach into the dishwasher and cut themselves because they didn't know there was a knife in there.

KEEP CHEMICALS AND FOOD SEPARATE: Make sure all the cleaning supplies are stored in a different location, away from the food. I keep all the soap and stuff under the sink and I never store food in there.

BE CAREFUL OF HOT THINGS! I assume the stove and the oven are always hot, so I always put my hand near it to see if I can feel any warmth. If it feels warm from a few inches away, it is probably really hot. Never touch the stove or the oven until you have tested it first.

IF THINGS GET GREASY, CLEAN UP: Lots of things in the kitchen can be greasy or oily. It's very important to wipe up anything messy as soon as you spill it. If I drop a slippery egg on the floor, I clean it up right away because I don't want anyone to step in it and then walk around getting egg everywhere. I also don't want anyone to slip and fall. After I clean up a mess, I wash my hands with soap and water—that's part of keeping a clean kitchen.

DON'T TRY TO DO TOO MUCH BY YOURSELF: Sometimes things are too heavy for me to lift by myself, so I always get one of my friends to help me. I don't want to drop and spill anything and I don't want to hurt myself lifting something too heavy for me. (Even though I am one of the strongest people I know, sometimes things are just too heavy or out of reach.)

FIRES HAPPEN: Always know where the fire extinguisher is. If there's a fire, yell and make sure an adult is coming, and never, never, never put water on a fire on the stove or in the oven. Flour or baking soda will stop a grease fire much faster, so I always know where those things are in my kitchen. Usually when I'm baking, I have cookbooks out and notebooks, too. I always keep anything made of paper away from the stove.

KEEP THE OVEN CLEAN: When I'm baking messy stuff like pies, I keep an extra sheet pan (also known as a rimmed baking sheet) on the bottom of the oven to catch anything that drips. If things drip all over the oven, it could eventually catch fire. So, if the oven ever gets messy, make sure to clean it up as soon as possible.

KITCHEN TOOLS AREN'T TOYS: There are lots of really interesting things in kitchens and they look like they would be fun to play with, but kitchen tools aren't toys, so be careful with everything.

WATER AND ELECTRICITY DON'T MIX: I like listening to music when I bake, but I always keep my electronics away from anything wet. I don't want my stuff to get ruined and I really don't want an electric shock!

SOAP AND WATER KILL GERMS: I have never made anyone sick from anything I have cooked because I always keep my kitchen super clean. I scrub the kitchen before and after I use it, so no germs find their way into my cookies. Treat the kitchen with respect and you'll have fun without accidents every single time.

· KITCHEN BASICS ·

The kitchen is where magic happens. The first thing to do is go into the kitchen with an adult and learn what everything is.

There's so many different kinds of tools and gadgets that do different things. I have a laser gun in my kitchen! And blow torches! I have weird spices from all over the world that bring smells and flavors from different countries right into my house. Get to know what all those things are and how they work. Learn how to turn the oven on and off. Try out the timer. Learn how the sink and the dishwasher work. If there's paper and mail and keys and shoes and junk in the kitchen, get it out of there. Look inside the fridge and freezer and see what's in there. If you don't know what something is called, look it up. You'll always learn something interesting. Kitchens are for exploring and creating and learning. Kitchens are where you make delicious things for the people you love to enjoy. That's a special thing, so treat the kitchen like the special place it is.

Here are some things that are good to know:

CRACKING EGGS: Always crack eggs on a flat surface, not the side of a bowl. This way the egg won't shatter and get shells into your dough or batter. When cracking eggs for a recipe, always crack them individually into a small bowl and then add them to the recipe. This way you can see if there's any shell that shouldn't be there.

SEPARATING EGGS: Get two bowls and a trash can. Crack the egg in the middle and break it into two halves. Holding the egg halves over a bowl, let the white drip out. Transfer the yolk back and forth between the halves, letting the white continue to drip out till it's all removed. Don't let any yolk get into the whites or you won't be able to whip the whites into meringue.

PREHEATING THE OVEN: You want the oven to be ready when you are, so turn the oven on before you start mixing so that whatever you intend to bake doesn't sit around. Most of the time, when it is time to bake, it is time to bake! If something has whipped air or baking powder in it and it sits around waiting for the oven to heat up, the batter or whatever you have will deflate.

COOLING STUFF: When things come out of the oven, most of the time you don't want to just stick them in the fridge and cool them down super fast. Get a cooling rack and let things cool on all sides at room temperature, nice and gentle. Cooling racks allow air to circulate all around your baked goods and keep the bottom from getting soggy.

BRINGING INGREDIENTS TO ROOM TEMPERATURE: Lots of times when you are baking, the temperature of the ingredients is really important. If you know you are going to bake tomorrow, read the recipe the day before and make sure that, if you need room temperature eggs or butter, you pull those ingredients out the night before, so they are ready for you. Don't worry, nothing will go bad.

TESTING IF SOMETHING IS DONE: If you want to know whether your brownies or cake is done, gently insert a bamboo skewer into it while it is in the oven. If you pull the skewer out and there's goo on it, it's not ready. If it comes out with only a few crumbs stuck to it, it's probably ready.

USING A STAND MIXER: Make sure the bowl is always clean and dry, and that you are using the right attachment for the job. Never mix too fast. Stand mixers are very powerful, so never stick anything in the bowl while the machine is on. You can get really hurt that way. Different recipes will call for different levels of whipped-ness. If something calls for stiff peaks, that means you want to whip your stuff until it doesn't jiggle when you shake it and has sharply defined folds in it. If something calls for soft peaks, it means to whip it only until it whips up and has volume but is still jiggly and soft with folds that slowly relax into themselves.

CUTTING STUFF: Always make sure there is a flat side to the items you want to chop, and that the flat side is down on the cutting board so whatever you are trying to cut doesn't roll around. Keep your fingers away from the knife edge. Curl your fingers around and keep the blade on your knuckles so you always know where the blade is. Cut slowly and carefully. As you get better and more confident, you can cut stuff like the pros. Practice!

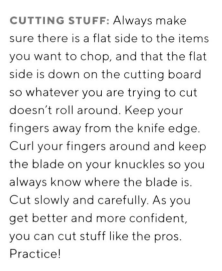

MAKING A DOUBLE BOILER: This is usually for melting chocolate. You can also melt chocolate in a microwave, but I don't trust anything that cooks with invisible death rays. Get a medium saucepot and a medium bowl. Put a few inches of water in the pot and turn on the heat until the water boils. Turn the heat down till the water is at a simmer and put the bowl on top of the pot. Put the chocolate in the bowl and watch it melt like magic.

CREAMING BUTTER AND SUGAR: This means you are beating the sugar and butter together so it gets smooth and airy. If you use room temperature butter, you'll see that the butter and sugar gets light and creamy and beautiful in a few minutes. Sometimes recipes will call for the whisk attachment in a stand mixer, but most of the time the best way to cream butter is with the paddle. Otherwise, a handheld mixer with beaters or hand mixing with a big ol' wooden spoon will do the trick.

PREPARING A PAN FOR BAKING: There are many ways to do this, and the recipe will usually tell you which one. Methods usually involve some kind of fat, either cooking spray or soft butter. Sometimes the recipe will call for parchment paper cut to the right size, or flour dusted onto the greased pan, or even both.

FOLDING: This is a term for mixing a batter very gently. Instead of sticking a wooden spoon in and just stirring like a monkey, folding is when you use a rubber spatula and gently fold a mixture over onto itself until it is just combined. Some recipes are very, very delicate and need to be handled gently. Like macarons.

SAUTÉING: To properly sauté, put a pan on the stove and turn on the heat. Wait until the pan is hot before adding butter or oil. Put whatever you are cooking into the pan and toss it around to coat it with the fat. Now, let what you are cooking cook. Don't keep flipping stuff around. It's fun to flip, but it bruises the food and keeps it from caramelizing.

TOASTING NUTS: Toast nuts dry (that is, with no fat) on a sheet pan in a preheated oven at 325°F for a few minutes. You will smell them when they are done. Nuts burn really easy, so don't walk away and always set a timer.

· EQUIPMENT ·

Let's look at the different tools in the kitchen and learn what they're for. Once you understand what everything is, baking is a lot easier and a lot more fun.

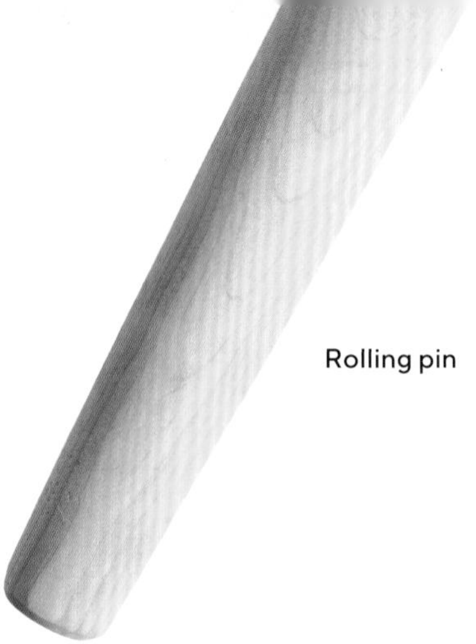

Rolling pin

Scissors

Measuring spoons

Muffin scoop

Cooling rack

Rubber Spatula

Grater

Bundt pan

Piping tips

Spreader

Wire whisk

Cookie cutters

Pizza cutter

Bamboo
skewers

Loaf pan

Squeeze
bottle

Metal tongs

Paint brush

Can
opener

Candy
thermometer

Pastry brush

Chef's knife

Measuring cups

9 × 13-inch baking pan

Microplane

Fine mesh
strainer

Paper cupcake
liner

Mixing bowl
(metal, ceramic)

Bench scraper

9-inch round
baking pan

Stand mixer with
paddle, whisk,
and dough-hook
attachments

Sauté pan

Digital scale

Ladle

Offset
spatulas

Chocolate
sixlets

Deli cup

Plastic
wrap

Parchment
paper

Wax
paper

Spoons

Metal spatula

Cupcake pan

Wooden
spoon

Ramekin

· INGREDIENTS ·

There are zillions of cool, interesting ingredients in baking.
Here are some of the most important ones:

BAKING SODA *AND* BAKING POWDER: Both of these things make breads, pastries, and cookies rise, but in different ways. The recipe will say one or the other or both, but remember they are not the same.

BUTTER: Butter is the fat from milk. If you whip cream too much, it separates into butter and buttermilk. I always use unsalted butter. Otherwise, I never how much salt is actually in the recipe. Also, there lots of fake "butters" out there, such as margarine. They don't usually work in baking, so if you want to substitute something for real butter, do some research on how to properly do that. I find that lots of substitute butters have weird melting points, which can make your finished baked goods come out dense or mushy.

BUTTERMILK: Always use nonfat buttermilk. Buttermilk is what is left over after you make butter. It is naturally low in fat.

CHOCOLATE: I know milk chocolate is more fun to eat, but most of the time you will want to bake with dark chocolate.

You don't need to bake with milk chocolate because most of the time you are adding milk and sugar anyways. Most of the time chocolate chips are fine, but sometimes you want a block of chocolate. Just read the recipe carefully, and it will tell you which to get.

COATING CHOCOLATE: Coating chocolate is different than regular chocolate. It comes in all kinds of colors and is made for melting and drying easily. Use it for any decorations you want to make. Real chocolate, also called *couverture*, melts easily but has to go through a very exact process called *tempering* to make it solidify again.

COCOA POWDER: There are two basic kinds of cocoa powder— natural and Dutch-process. Natural cocoa powder is lighter in color and is more acidic while Dutch-process cocoa powder is darker and richer. If you don't know which to use, read the recipe. If the recipe calls for baking powder, use Dutch-process cocoa powder. If the recipe calls for baking soda, use natural cocoa powder. If both soda and powder are in the ingredients, err on the side of natural cocoa when there's more soda than powder. When there's more powder than soda, use Dutch-process.

COOKING SPRAY: This keeps things from sticking to your pans. I use Vegelene brand.

EGGS: I bake with grade A large eggs. There are a few different sizes, but large eggs are the most common. The egg whites are how we make meringue. Always open the carton of eggs at the store and make sure none of the eggs are broken. Sometimes eggs are dirty and have "chicken stuff" on them. I like to wash it off. Lots of my recipes call for room temperature eggs. These mix into a batter more easily and help avoid overmixing. You can use cold eggs—just mix slow and be careful not to overmix.

FLOUR: There's all kinds of flours out there. Most of the time you will be using all-purpose flour. It's good for most things. Chewier things like breads and bagels use bread flour. Light, delicate things use cake or pastry flour. Recipes will always tell you which one to use. If you're gluten sensitive, I like to use Cup4Cup flour. It should work for most, if not all, of these recipes.

FOOD COLORING: There are lots of different kinds. Experiment and see which ones you like. There are thick gel colors that are really strong and there's thinner ones that are watery and weak. I like the gel colors, so I know I'm not adding any water to my recipe that is not

supposed to be there. There's also a much greater variety in the colors you can get when using gels.

MARZIPAN: Marzipan is a finely ground almond paste with more than 50 percent sugar as its ingredients. It's a really fun thing to sculpt with and airbrush.

MILK: Skim, 1%, 2%, whole, half-and-half, and heavy cream—it's all milk. The different names are just how much milk fat is in that particular milk. Always use the milk that a recipe calls for. If a recipe calls for heavy cream and you use skim milk, there won't be enough fat in the recipe and whatever it is will be dry and weird. Also, there are lots of plant-based "milks" out there. That's cool and all, but when you use them for baking, you are basically just adding water, not milk.

MOLASSES: Molasses is what makes brown sugar brown. There are two different kinds of molasses: blackstrap and true molasses. If you can find true molasses, get it. If not, blackstrap is fine, it is just a little more bitter and robust.

NUTS: Some nuts come toasted and some come raw. Always toast your nuts, unless they are sitting on top of something in the oven, then they will toast while whatever is baking.

OIL: There's lots of different kinds, but for baking, usually this just means canola or vegetable oil.

SALT: I use only kosher salt because table salt has iodine in it, and iodine tastes like caca. I put a pinch of salt in everything. Kosher salt has a neutral flavor; it's just salt. Using salt is really important in desserts because if something is just sweet and has no salt, it will have no balance. Like listening to music with one ear, it just doesn't have dimension.

SANDING SUGAR: This is the big crunchy sugar on top of cookies and muffins. It doesn't melt in the oven. It's sometimes called coarse sugar.

SPICES: Make sure that all your spices are reasonably fresh. Two-year-old cinnamon that has been sitting in your cupboard will never taste as good as freshly ground cinnamon.

SPRINKLES: Add sprinkles to almost anything to make it more fun: cookies, cakes, ice cream, whatever. Just make sure to add the sprinkles at the *end* of the mixing process so they don't melt and make everything gray. Sprinkles are sometimes referred to as Jimmies.

SUGAR: There's lots of different kinds of sugar. Powdered sugar (also called 10X or confectioner's sugar) is bright white and really soft. Sanding sugar can be any color and is coarse and grainy. Most recipes call for granulated sugar, which is white and looks like really fine sand. There's light brown sugar, which has molasses in it. Dark brown sugar has lots of molasses in it. Superfine sugar is just regular sugar but with much smaller crystals for when you need sugar to dissolve really fast.

VANILLA: Vanilla beans taste the best, but pure vanilla extract is almost as good. Imitation vanilla extract, sometimes called "vanillin," is gnarly. If you get real vanilla beans, slice them the long way in half and, using the tip of the knife, carefully scrape out the tiny black seeds into whatever you are baking. If you want the seeds but can't find fresh vanilla beans, you can use vanilla bean paste.

ZEST: This is the outer layer of the skin (or peel) of a citrus fruit. Make sure you're only using the part that is colored. The white part underneath is bitter and doesn't taste nice.

DECORATING TECHNIQUES

If you're going to spend a good amount of time making something delicious, you should also make it look nice. Here are a few things you can do to dress up your cakes and pastries.

CRUMB-COATING A CAKE: Place your stacked and filled cake onto a cake turntable. If you don't have a cake turntable, use the back of a round plate. Spread a thin layer of buttercream over the whole cake with a metal spatula. Next, take a bench scraper and make the iced side of the cake perfectly flat and really thin. To ice the top, using a metal spatula, pull the frosting from the cake edge into the middle to give the cake a nice sharp foundation for the final icing. Don't mix this buttercream, which has crumbs in it, with the fresh buttercream that doesn't. Put the crumb-coated cake in the fridge to allow the buttercream to set up.

DUSTING WITH POWDERED SUGAR: I have a dedicated shaker for powdered sugar, but that's because I bake all the time. You don't need to do that. To make a nice dusting of powdered sugar, put some powdered sugar into a fine-mesh strainer. Holding your free hand still over whatever you want to dust, gently tap the strainer against your hand. Don't tap your hand against the strainer. I don't why, it just works better to tap the strainer.

ICING A CAKE: Start with freshly paddled room temperature buttercream. To get those nice smooth, straight sides, smear a generous amount of buttercream all over the crumb-coated cake. Using a bench scraper, smooth out the sides of the cake, making sure to hold the bench scraper exactly perpendicular to the cake turntable or table. Also make sure that plenty of buttercream travels up the side of the cake to rest about an inch *above* the top of the cake. Next, use an icing spatula to smooth out the top, starting from the edge and working your way in to the center.

MAKING CORNETS: These are little tiny piping bags made out of a triangular piece of parchment paper. Cut an unequal right triangle and, starting at the least acute angle, roll it into a cone with a sharp tip. Fold down the remaining edge of parchment over the lip of the base of the cone, and you have a nice little piping bag that is much easier to control than a big plastic bag. Fill it halfway with ganache, melted chocolate, or royal icing, fold the back up so your goo doesn't come out, and cut a tiny hole at the tip of the bag. You are ready to pipe some really thin lines.

MAKING GANACHE: There are different ratios of chocolate and cream for making different kinds of ganache. For a cake filling or a thick glaze, make a 1:1 ganache, or one part cream to one part chocolate. For a thick ganache that you can roll into truffles, make a 1:2 ganache of one part cream to two parts chocolate. To make a ganache you can pour over a cake, make a 2:1 ganache, or two parts cream to one part chocolate. To make any ganache, pour the cream into a saucepan and bring it to a boil. Put the chocolate (either as chips or chopped into small pieces) into a bowl and pour the hot cream over the chocolate. Cover the bowl with a kitchen towel and wait a few minutes for the chocolate to melt. When the chocolate has melted, whisk until the ganache is smooth and shiny.

MAKING ROYAL ICING: Put 4 cups of powdered sugar in a big bowl. Add 2 egg whites to the bowl (see Separating Eggs in Kitchen Basics, page 9) and whip it like crazy. If you want it thinner, add more egg. If you want it thicker, add more sugar. To store royal icing so it doesn't get a hard skin, place it into a storage container. Place a moist (not wet) paper towel directly onto the surface of the icing. Cover the container with a tight-fitting lid or plastic wrap and store at room temperature. I like to make fresh royal icing every time I use it. Don't keep it for more than 24 hours.

PIPING A BORDER: Insert your preferred tip into a plastic piping bag. With freshly paddled buttercream at room temperature, fill the piping bag about halfway. Twist the back of the bag so the buttercream doesn't come out the wrong end. Start piping by placing the tip where you want the icing decoration to be, then apply pressure with your hand, but don't move the bag. Let the decoration build while the bag is stationary. When the decoration is the size you want, simultaneously pull the bag away and *slowly* decrease the pressure so you get a smooth release. Repeat all the way around the cake.

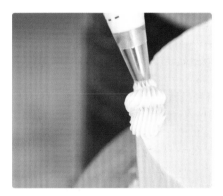

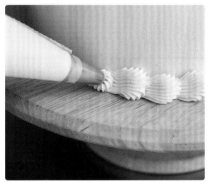

STACKING AND FILLING A CAKE: First, cut a piece of cardboard the exact circumference of your cake and place the bottom layer, cut side up, onto the cardboard. If you want your cakes to be nice and flat on the top, cut the domes off of each layer before you stack them. Then, starting with the first cake, with the cut side up, spread your filling (jam, buttercream, curd, chocolate, etc.). Place the next cake, if it is going to be the top layer, cut side down. If it's not the top layer, it doesn't matter. Basically, whichever layer is going to be the top, stack it cut side down. This way, you have the baked side facing out, which is much easier to ice than the cut side.

WHIPPING CREAM: To make whipped cream, start with really cold whipping cream (or heavy cream). If you want to put the bowl and the whisk in the fridge as well, it makes whipping cream easier and faster. Whip cream at medium speed. Too fast and you make a mess, and the whipped cream is less stable. To make your whipped cream real stable, add a few tablespoons of soft, room temperature cream cheese to the cream before you whip it. Also, whipped cream doesn't need much sugar at all. I use powdered sugar and a pinch of kosher salt. Make your whipped cream as sweet as you want. You're the chef.

FOR THE LOVE OF STREUSEL: This is the crumbly stuff on top of muffins, crumbles, and buckles. Basically, streusel is a combination of butter, sugar, and flour, with spices and other stuff thrown in for flavor and texture. There are millions of streusel recipes with things like nuts, oats, coconut, cocoa, ground cinnamon, and brown sugar. They're really easy to make, so try a few and see what you like.

MAKING COULIS: A coulis is a nice sweet, fruity sauce, usually made with berries. Start by sprinkling a little sugar onto your fruit and letting it sit for about 30 minutes. Not too much sugar, just enough to thinly cover the fruit. This is called *macerating* and makes all the water in the fruit turn into fruit syrup. Next, pour the fruit into a blender and pulse until it is smooth. Strain out any seeds.

· BEFORE YOU START ·

All right, you know what your ingredients are.
You know how the oven works. It's almost time to bake!
Just a few more tips and you'll be ready to go.

READ YOUR RECIPE: Make sure you understand the order in which everything should be done. Go through the ingredients and make sure you have everything you need. It's good to be able to anticipate next steps, so you know what's coming around the corner.

MAKE SURE THERE IS SPACE IN YOUR REFRIGERATOR: Sometimes you need to be able to put a sheet pan in the fridge. Or a big bowl of cookie dough. Make sure there is room.

ALWAYS MAKE EXTRA! You know you're gonna eat some.

TAKE NOTES: Write things down, directly in this book or in a notebook. Sometimes you will want to change a recipe or make a note for the next time you make something. Write it down so you don't forget.

A LITTLE EXTRA ISN'T ALWAYS BETTER: Most recipes call for a specific amount of stuff. It's usually a good idea to follow the recipe. If there wasn't enough cinnamon to your liking, make a note to add more to the recipe next time.

TASTY, DELICIOUS, TOTALLY TRICKED-OUT TREATS

YOUR IMAGINATION IS THE ONLY LIMIT to what you can achieve. This is true for pretty much everything, but especially in baking. The first step in how to create *anything* is learning how to create *something*. That's where this book comes in. Here's a bunch of recipes—some are relatively easy, some are more difficult. Baking takes practice. I've been baking for...a long time, and I'm still figuring it out, which is what makes baking so much fun for me. There's always something new to learn. But you will find that as you learn, using your imagination will get easier and your baking will get better. If you want to make a rainbow unicorn laser cookie with chocolate mermaid tails and sugar dragon wings, you can, but first you have to learn how to make a cookie. I designed this book with lots of basic recipes that bakers of every age should learn how to do, and then there are ideas and methods for tricking out lots of those recipes. You'll learn how to make a few different kinds of cookies, and then you'll learn how to make ice-cream sandwiches or cookie milkshakes or cream pies with any cookies, not just the ones in this book. I want you to be able to see the possibilities of everything in the kitchen. Think of recipes like a coloring book. At first, there is a line drawing of something, and you use crayons and markers and pencils and stuff to fill in the spaces. Soon, you get good at that and you start adding backgrounds and your own details to the picture, and before you know it, you aren't using coloring books anymore, you are using big, white pieces of paper and drawing anything you can think of. The lines in the coloring book are just helping you learn how to use crayons and markers. Once you know how to use them, you make your own lines. The important thing is learning how.

Whether you are trying out baking for the first time or you're trying out for the *Kids Baking Championship* (or even if you wish you were trying out for *KBC* but you missed the cutoff by a year or twenty), you can use this book. Flip through the pages, read the recipes, and look at the pictures. What looks good to you? What do you wanna eat? Maybe there is a recipe in here that calls for chocolate chips. Maybe you wanna use butterscotch chips. I say go for it, see what happens. Try it, see what you think, and most importantly, *write it down*. I give you permission to write in this book. If you try a recipe and you want to make a change, write down the changes in pencil and try it again. If it works, write it down in ink. If it doesn't, erase it.

Every recipe will have a list of ingredients and a list of special equipment that you will need to make it. Always read the recipes first all the way through and make sure that you have everything you need. Make yourself a shopping list and look through the kitchen before you go to the store to make sure you are only buying what you need. If you buy baking powder every time you make muffins, you are going to have lots of baking powder.

Remember, baking well means doing lots of small, easy things correctly. It isn't 'Nam—there are rules. Follow the rules. Baseball wouldn't be nearly as fun if everyone broke the rules. I know that following rules can seem boring or pointless sometimes, but the rules are there because somebody figured them out. Not following the rules can seem like fun, but when the goal is to make something delicious, following the rules is very important. And also, the better you get at baking, and the more you understand the rules, the more you can bend them.

All the recipes in this book are written down by weight as well as volume, which is why everything is written in grams and tablespoons. Professional bakers read and write recipes by weight because because weighing your ingredients is faster, cleaner, and much more accurate than using cups and spoons. Learn the correct way when you are young, and you'll do it right your whole life. There are a few volume measurements for some things that are very small, and that's fine. When a recipe calls for cups and spoons, I weigh the ingredients as I'm making it and I write down what the weights are. You can get a digital scale online or even at the grocery store for really cheap. The other nice thing about weighing out ingredients is that it is much easier to do the math if you want to make larger batches.

Math? Yup, there is lots of math in baking. There is chemistry and physics. There is geometry. There is lots of measuring and problem solving. You know when you are in class and you wonder why anyone learns math? Baking. You learn math because you want delicious pies and cookies. When you put baking soda into a recipe, the baking soda reacts with the acid in the recipe and makes it rise. It's a chemical reaction! That's science. Isn't that cool?

So, pick a recipe. Read it. Make sure you have everything you need to make it. Then clean the kitchen, weigh out your ingredients, preheat the oven, and make some tricked-out treats.

PEACE, DUFF

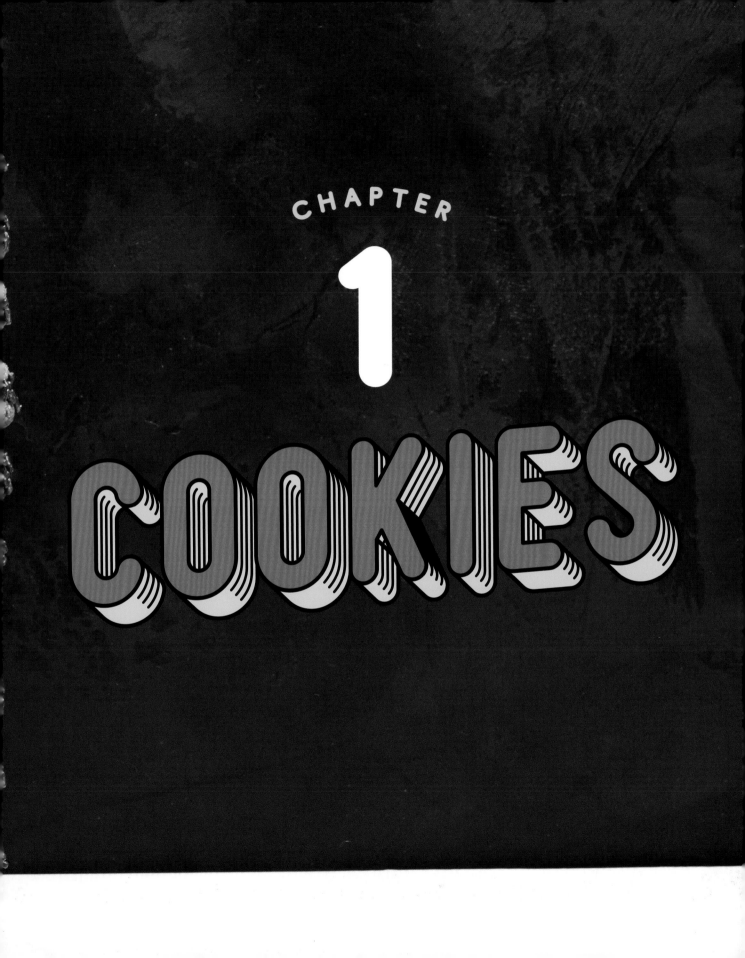

CHAPTER

1

COOKIES

COOKIES

MAKES

24

cookies

There are some things in life that are good to know. How to tie your shoe. How to find a bathroom in another country. But more important than any of those is knowing how to make a good chocolate chip cookie.

PREP TIME
10 minutes
BAKING TIME
8 to 12 minutes

Ingredients

1 cup (2 sticks or 226 grams) unsalted butter, room temperature

¾ cups (150 grams) granulated sugar

¾ cups (139 grams) lightly packed light brown sugar

1 teaspoon (6 grams) kosher salt

2 large eggs

1 teaspoon (5 grams) pure vanilla extract

2¼ cups (338 grams) all-purpose flour

1 teaspoon (6 grams) baking soda

2 cups (350 grams) semisweet chocolate chips

EQUIPMENT

- **Parchment paper**
- **Stand mixer**
- **Spatula**
- **Medium bowl**
- **Whisk**
- **Muffin scoop**
- **Sheet pan**
- **Cooling rack**

RECIPE CONTINUES

1. Preheat the oven to 375°F. Line a sheet pan with parchment paper.

2. In the bowl of a stand mixer fitted with the paddle attachment, cream the butter, sugar, brown sugar, and salt together on medium speed until it's light and fluffy.

3. Add the eggs and vanilla and mix to incorporate.

4. Scrape the sides of the bowl with a rubber spatula and then mix for another 30 seconds.

5. In a separate medium bowl, whisk together the flour and the baking soda. Add the flour mixture to the creamed butter, and mix everything together on medium-low speed till combined. Take the bowl off the mixer.

6. Add the chocolate chips and, using the rubber spatula, mix together gently by hand.

7. Scoop 1½-inch balls of cookie dough and place them about 3 inches apart on your sheet pan.

8. Bake for 8 to 12 minutes.

9. Let the cookies cool for 5 minutes, then transfer them to a cooling rack until they're ready to eat.

Duff's Tip

You can make this dough ahead of time and keep it in the fridge for up to a week or in the freezer for 6 to 8 months.

ICE-CREAM COOKIE SANDWICHES

It's good to know how to make an ice-cream cookie sandwich. I have a friend who loves them so much that he'll do anything I want if I give him one. Sometimes I can't get to the store to get him one, so I have to make them from scratch. But then again, from scratch is better anyway.

So, the first thing you need to do is make some space in your freezer for a plate of cookies. Whenever the cookies you want to use are cool, freeze them for at least an hour. Next, scoop out your ice cream (and remember, you can use any kind of ice cream you want) and place the ice cream on the flat side of a cookie. Put the top cookie on top, smush it until the ice cream is level with the edge of the cookies, and put the sandwich in the freezer for 20 minutes.

Next, get a bowl that is big enough to fit the whole sandwich into it and fill it with chopped, toasted nuts, mini chocolate chips, or sprinkles. Remove the sandwiches from the freezer and roll the edges in the topping. Put the sandwiches back in the freezer for 10 minutes, then wrap them in plastic wrap. Keep the sandwiches in the freezer until your own ice-cream-cookie-sandwich-loving friends come over.

CONFETTI
· SNICKERDOODLES ·

MAKES
24
cookies

I'm a crispy cookie kinda guy, but these chewy snickerdoodles are righteous. There is a firm airiness to them that makes these cookies a joy to eat. Sometimes, it's not the flavor of something that makes it delicious, it's the texture.

PREP TIME
10 minutes, plus 15 minutes for chilling
BAKING TIME
15 to 18 minutes

Ingredients

FOR THE COOKIE DOUGH

½ cup (1 stick or 113 grams) unsalted butter, room temperature

¾ cup (150 grams) granulated sugar

1 large egg

1 teaspoon (5 grams) pure vanilla extract

1⅓ cups (200 grams) all-purpose flour

1 teaspoon (4 grams) cream of tartar

½ teaspoon (3 grams) baking soda

Pinch of kosher salt

2½ tablespoons of rainbow sprinkles

FOR THE CINNAMON SUGAR

¼ cup (50 grams) granulated sugar

1 tablespoon (7 grams) ground cinnamon

EQUIPMENT

- Stand mixer
- 2 medium bowls
- Whisk
- Parchment paper
- Sheet pan
- Small bowl
- Spatula

RECIPE CONTINUES ➤

1. In the bowl of a stand mixer fitted with the paddle attachment, cream the butter and sugar on medium-high until the mixture is light and fluffy.

2. Add the egg and vanilla, then mix to combine.

3. In a separate medium bowl, whisk together flour, cream of tartar, baking soda, and salt. Add the flour mixture to the butter mixture and combine on low speed until a nice dough forms, about 3 minutes.

4. Add the sprinkles and mix for a few more seconds to incorporate, but be careful not to mix too long or else the paddle will crush the sprinkles.

5. Transfer the dough to a medium bowl, then refrigerate for 15 minutes.

6. Preheat the oven to 350°F. Cover two sheet pans with parchment.

7. Roll the chilled dough into 1- to 2-inch balls and then roll the balls in a small bowl of ground cinnamon sugar, completely coating them.

8. Arrange the coated balls on the sheet pans about 3 inches apart so the cookies can spread without running into each other.

9. Bake for 15 to 18 minutes, until the cookies start to brown. Cool the cookies on a cooling rack before eating.

Duff's Tip

Wash your hands! You're going to be rolling cookies with your bare hands. Anything that's stuck to your hands will stick to the cookies. I don't wanna eat anything that was stuck to your hands. So wash them.

9 THINGS
YOU CAN DO WITH STORE-BOUGHT COOKIES

If you don't have time to bake your own cookies but you're bored by plain old store-bought cookies, here are some creative ways you can use those cookies as ingredients for something even more amazing.

1 COOKIE-STUFFED BROWNIES Make a brownie batter (see the brownie recipe in Stuffed-Crust Dessert Pizza on page 99) and fill muffin cups about halfway. Then shove in your favorite cookie so it is surrounded by brownie batter. These bake fast, in about 10 minutes or according to your brownie recipe, so watch them.

2 COOKIE PUDDING POPS Put your cookies in the cup of a blender and add a box of instant pudding mix. Follow the directions on the pudding box for how much liquid to add, then blend away. You can also add some fresh fruit to the blender. Pour the mixture into popsicle molds and freeze for about 4 hours.

3 ICEBOX COOKIE CAKE In an 8-inch square pan, layer whipped cream and cookies, then set in the fridge for a few hours. I like whipped cream with Nutter Butters and butterscotch chips.

4 COOKIE MILKSHAKE Blend your favorite cookies with your favorite ice cream, malt powder, and milk.

5 COOKIE BARK Chop up your favorite cookies, toss with melted chocolate, and cool on a sheet pan.

6 KRISPY KOOKIE TREATS Crush up cookies and toss into your favorite rice crispy treat recipe.

7 COOKIE POPS Crush up your favorite cookies into a paste. If they are dry cookies, add some buttercream, peanut butter, or something gooey. Roll the paste into 1-inch balls, dip them in melted chocolate, decorate with sprinkles, and add a stick if you want. If not, call it a cookie truffle.

8 COOKIE FUDGE Make the fudge recipe on page 94 and toss crushed cookies in the bowl before you allow the fudge to set.

9 COOKIE SURPRISE Make the dough from the Classic Chocolate Chip Cookies recipe on page 29 and press it around some other kind of cookie. Mind = blown.

PEANUT BUTTER

• COOKIE SANDWICHES •

MAKES
20 to 25
cookie sandwiches

So, the thing about peanut butter cookies is that peanut butter cookies are awesome. Peanut butter is delicious. Cookies are delicious. Peanut butter cookies are therefore twice as delicious as any other cookie. That's just science. These cookies are really great just by themselves with a big glass of cold milk but, if you want extra, fill 'em up! You can put chocolate ganache inside, or anything you want.

PREP TIME
COOKIES:
30 minutes, plus 30 minutes for chilling
GANACHE:
15 minutes, plus 1 hour for chilling
BAKING TIME
10 minutes

Ingredients

FOR THE GANACHE

8 ounces (227 grams) semisweet chocolate chips

8 ounces (227 grams) heavy cream

FOR THE COOKIES

½ cup (1 stick or 113 grams) soft, room temperature butter

1 cup (200 grams) granulated sugar (plus more sugar for rolling)

1 tablespoon (40 grams) blackstrap molasses

½ cup plus 2 tablespoons (160 grams) crunchy peanut butter (you can use smooth peanut butter, but...why?)

1½ teaspoons (7 grams) pure vanilla extract

1 large egg

½ teaspoon (2 grams) baking powder

½ teaspoon (3 grams) baking soda

Pinch of kosher salt

1 cup plus 2 tablespoons (170 grams) all-purpose flour

FOR DECORATING

Chocolate sprinkles

EQUIPMENT

- 2 medium bowls
- 1 small saucepan
- Kitchen towel
- Whisk
- Parchment paper
- 2 sheet pans
- Stand mixer
- Rubber spatula
- 2 small bowls
- 1 or 2 plastic piping bags
- 1 or 2 medium plain piping tip
- Paper towels
- Fork
- Cooling rack

RECIPE CONTINUES →

MAKE THE GANACHE

1 Put the chocolate chips in a medium bowl and set aside.

2 Pour the cream into a small saucepan and, over medium-high heat, bring the cream to a boil.

3 Turn off the heat and pour the cream over the chocolate. Cover the bowl with a kitchen towel and let it sit for 3 minutes.

4 Remove the towel and whisk the ganache until it's shiny.

5 Put the ganache in the fridge for about an hour and let it cool.

MAKE THE COOKIE DOUGH

6 Measure all the ingredients. (Remember mise en place from page 7.) In the bowl of a stand mixer using the paddle attachment, cream the butter, sugar, and molasses until it is fluffy.

7 When the sound of the mixer changes from a *slop slop slop* to *fwap fwap fwap*, add the peanut butter, vanilla, and egg. Mix until it is all the same color.

8 Scrape the sides of the bowl with a rubber spatula and mix for another 30 seconds.

9 Take the bowl off the mixer and add the baking powder, baking soda, salt, and flour. Use a rubber spatula to mix the cookie batter, scraping the sides of the bowl a lot. It's better for the cookies and it's way more fun to mix it by hand.

10 Transfer the cookie dough to a medium bowl, cover with a kitchen towel, and put it in the fridge for 30 minutes.

11 Wash the mixer bowl and rubber spatula.

TO FINISH THE GANACHE

12 Take the cooled chocolate ganache out of the fridge and transfer it to the bowl of the stand mixer.

13 Using the wire whisk attachment, whip the ganache until it is a creamy, light brown color and real fluffy. (Remember, from *slop slop* to *fwap fwap*.)

14 Using a rubber spatula, load the ganache into a piping bag prepared with a medium plain tip. (If you need to, use two piping bags so you don't overfill the bags.)

15 Tie a twist tie around the back of the bag so the ganache doesn't shoot out the back.

16 Put the bag in the fridge for 1 hour.

TO BAKE THE COOKIES

17 Preheat the oven to 375°F. Line two sheet pans with parchment paper. Make a paper towel moist with water.

18 Set up a cookie rolling station with the parchment-covered sheet pans, a small bowl of sugar, the chilled cookie dough, and the moist paper towel.

19 Put your hands on the moist towel to get them just slightly damp. Not wet, just moist.

20 Roll a ball of dough till it's a little smaller than a golf ball.

21 Drop the ball into the sugar so just half of the ball gets covered.

22 Put the ball on the sheet pan, sugar side down. Remoisten your hands and repeat until you have used all the dough. (Keep the balls of dough at least 3 inches apart! They'll spread when they bake and mess each other up.)

23 Using a fork, press gently on each cookie twice to make a crisscross pattern.

24 Bake for 10 minutes or *just* right before they start to turn brown on the tips of the crisscross pattern.

25 Carefully remove the sheet pan from the oven and let the cookies cool on the pan. (You want the bottoms of the cookies to be a bit more done than the tops.)

26 Let them cool completely before making your sandwiches!

TO FINISH THE COOKIES

27 Fill a small bowl with chocolate sprinkles and tear a piece of parchment large enough to hold up to 25 cookie sandwiches. Wash your hands.

28 Pipe a mound of ganache about the size of a quarter onto one cookie. Be careful not to pipe too much! I promise, your cookies will be better with less ganache than you think.

29 Place another cookie on top of the ganache and gently press the cookies together until the ganache is exactly level with the outside edge of the cookies.

30 Roll the cookie sandwich in the sprinkles so the sprinkles stick to the ganache.

31 Let finished cookie sandwiches rest on the parchment paper. Store them in an airtight container for up to 5 days.

Duff's Tip

Leave a little ganache showing around the edge so you can roll your sandwich cookies in sprinkles.

COOKIE SANDWICHES

Cookies are good. Cookie sandwiches are better. Instead of a cookie, you get two cookies and a yummy filling. Bonus, right? Here are some good cookie sandwich fillings.

CREAMY WHITE
COOKIE-SANDWICH FILLING

2⅓ cups (280 grams) powdered sugar

½ cup (95 grams) vegetable shortening

1 teaspoon (5 grams) pure vanilla extract

2 teaspoons cold water

Pinch of kosher salt

In the bowl of a stand mixer using the paddle attachment, mix everything together.

PEANUT BUTTER
COOKIE-SANDWICH FILLING

1½ cups (180 grams) powdered sugar

3 ounces (85 grams) creamy peanut butter

3 tablespoons (45 grams) heavy cream

¼ cup (30 grams) chopped, roasted, salted, or unsalted peanuts

In the bowl of a stand mixer fitted with the paddle attachment, cream everything together except for the peanuts. Fold in the peanuts.

CREAM CHEESE
COOKIE-SANDWICH FILLING

4 ounces (113 grams) cream cheese, at room temperature

6 tablespoons (85 grams grams) butter, at room temperature

Pinch of kosher salt

½ teaspoon (3 grams) pure vanilla extract

1 ½ cups (180grams) powdered sugar

In the bowl of a stand mixer fitted with the paddle attachment, cream everything together.

MARSHMALLOW CREAM
COOKIE-SANDWICH FILLING

½ cup (1 stick or 113 grams) butter, at room temperature

1 (7 ½-ounce) jar marshmallow cream

1 cup (120 grams) powdered sugar

½ teaspoon (3 grams) pure vanilla extract

Pinch of kosher salt

Heavy cream (if needed)

In the bowl of a stand mixer fitted with the paddle attachment, cream everything together.

Note

If marshmallow cream is too thick, add a few drops of heavy cream at a time until it looks right. You want it spreadable but not so loose it drips out of the mixing bowl.

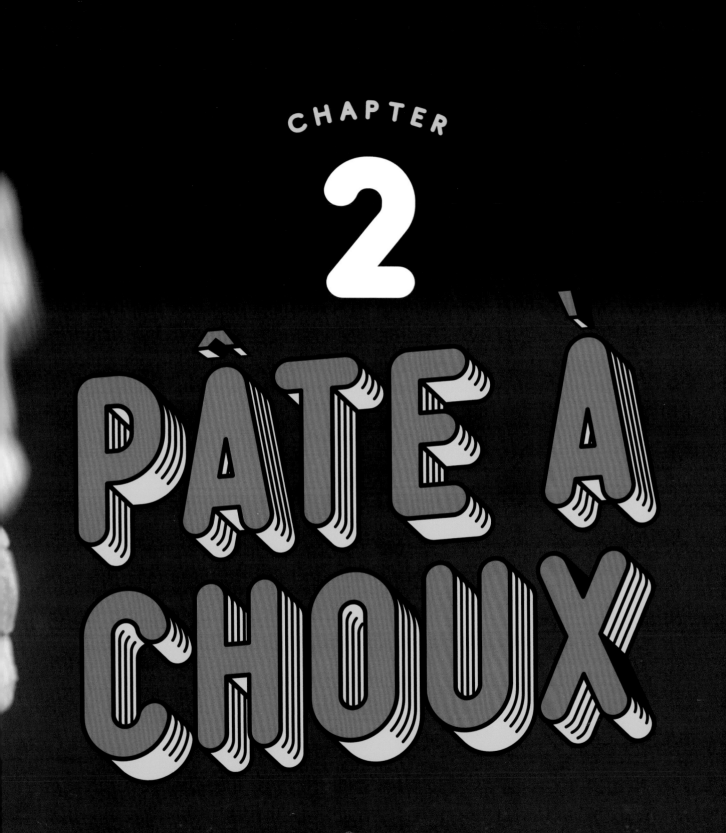

CHAPTER

2

PÂTE À CHOUX

BLITZ PUFF PASTRY

MAKES

1

10-inch dessert pizza or various amount of other items

Traditional puff pastries can take a loooong time to make and are really tricky to get right. Blitz puff pastries, on the other hand, use a fast-and-easy dough that tastes just as good. This dough freezes well, so you can whip up a few batches and keep them in the freezer so you have them ready whenever you're jonesing for some puff pastry deliciousness.

PREP TIME
15 minutes, plus 40 minutes for resting

INGREDIENTS

1½ cups plus 2 tablespoons (240 grams) all-purpose flour, plus more for dusting

½ teaspoon (3 grams) kosher salt

½ teaspoon (2 grams) baking powder

1 cup (2 sticks or 226 grams) cold unsalted butter, cut into small cubes

½ cup plus 2 tablespoons (150 grams) cold sour cream

EQUIPMENT

• **Large bowl**
• **Whisk**
• **Rubber spatula**
• **Sheet pan**
• **Plastic wrap**

In a large bowl, whisk together the flour, salt, and baking powder.

Toss the butter in the flour mix so each butter piece gets coated. Using your fingers, rub the butter into the flour just a bit.

Stir in the sour cream with a rubber spatula.

When the dough is thick, turn it out onto a floured surface and knead it gently and quickly three times.

Shape the dough into a rough rectangle, flour both sides of it, and roll it out until it's about ½ to ¾ inch thick.

Fold the dough into thirds, like a tourist brochure you get in the lobby of a motel.

Wrap the folded dough in plastic wrap and refrigerate for 40 minutes.

Remove from the fridge and then shape, roll, fold in thirds again, and refrigerate.

The dough is ready to use or can be frozen for up to 20 weeks.

PÂTE À CHOUX

MAKES 36 round puffs

Pâte à choux (prounounced PAT-a-SHOO) is a crispy-on-the-outside, buttery-on-the-inside vehicle for sweet, creamy stuff. And it's hollow, so you can fit a lot of that sweet, creamy stuff inside it. Baking pâte à choux is also really interesting. The water in the dough turns to steam in the oven and makes the dough puff up. When you make this pâte à choux, keep the oven light on 'cause it's fun to watch it bake.

PREP TIME 15 minutes

INGREDIENTS

1½ cups (354 grams) water

1 stick plus 1 tablespoon (127 grams) unsalted butter

1 teaspoon (5 grams) granulated sugar

1 teaspoon (6 grams) kosher salt

1⅓ cups (200 grams) all-purpose flour

6 large eggs

EQUIPMENT

- **Large saucepan**
- **Wooden spoon**
- **Stand mixer**

In a large saucepan, combine the water, butter, sugar, and salt with a wooden spoon. Heat on high till just before it boils. Turn the heat down to a simmer. Add the flour and stir until a dough forms, about 2 to 3 minutes.

Transfer the dough into the bowl of a stand mixer with the paddle attachment. Beat the dough on low speed until no more steam comes out of the bowl.

Change mixing speed to medium-low and beat in one egg at a time. Keep mixing until the dough just about starts to settle by itself but not quite. Add each egg and mix thoroughly. After 4 eggs, stop the mixer and watch the dough. You want the dough to be slightly mushy but still hold its shape. You might not use all 6 eggs.

The dough is now ready to be baked. You can also store pâte à choux in the fridge for up to 3 days or freeze it for up to 3 months.

• NEAPOLITAN PROFITEROLE •

SUNDAE

MAKES

8

sundaes

Neapolitan means some kind of combination of vanilla, chocolate, and strawberry. These three flavors really go well together. The vanilla is kind of floral, the chocolate is just chocolatey, and the strawberries are tart and fruity. When you combine all those flavors, each one complements the other two and creates a whole new flavor experience.

PREP TIME
45 minutes

BAKING TIME
20 to 24 minutes

Ingredients

FOR THE PROFITEROLES

1 recipe Pâte à choux (page 45)

1 quart of your favorite vanilla bean ice cream

FOR THE HOT FUDGE SAUCE

2 cups (520 grams) heavy cream

4 tablespoons (½ stick or 57 grams) unsalted butter

½ cup (90 grams) lightly packed light brown sugar

¾ cup (150 grams) granulated sugar

Pinch of kosher salt

2 ounces (59 grams) bittersweet chocolate chips

1¼ cups (147 grams) Dutch-process cocoa powder

½ teaspoon (3 grams) pure vanilla extract

FOR THE WHIPPED CREAM

4 ounces (113 grams) cream cheese, room temperature

1½ cups (375 grams) heavy cream

½ cup (10 grams) freeze-dried strawberries, crushed into a powder

¼ cup (31 grams) powdered sugar

Pinch of kosher salt

FOR THE GANACHE

6 ounces (170 grams) semisweet chocolate

6 ounces (170 grams) heavy cream

1 jar Luxardo maraschino cherries

1 quart vanilla ice cream

EQUIPMENT

- Rubber spatula
- Piping bag
- Medium or large plain tip
- 2 sheet pans
- Parchment paper
- Medium saucepan
- Stand mixer
- Medium bowl
- Whisk
- Kitchen towel
- Knife
- Cutting board

RECIPE CONTINUES →

MAKE THE PROFITEROLES

1 Preheat the oven to 400°F.

2 Using a rubber spatula, put the pâte à choux into a piping bag fitted with a medium or large plain tip.

3 Pipe a tiny dot of pâte à choux on each corner of two sheet pans.

4 Line the two sheet pans with parchment paper and press the corners into the pâte à choux so the parchment doesn't flop around when you pipe balls of dough on it.

5 Hold the piping bag about a centimeter above the parchment. Don't move the bag. Holding the bag steady and in place, pipe out a mound of pâte à choux. Let the mound build, without moving the piping bag, into a golf ball.

6 When your pâte à choux is the size of a golf ball, stop squeezing and flick the tip really fast to try to creating a clean break and smooth top. (If you get a little horn or peak on the top, dip your finger in water and gently smooth it down.)

7 Repeat until the sheet pan is covered with golf balls of pâte à choux about 2 inches apart from each other.

8 Bake for 10 to 12 minutes until they are just beginning to turn brown, then turn the oven down to 350°F and bake for another 10 to 12 minutes until the profiteroles feel crispy and hollow.

9 Remove the pans from the oven and set aside to cool.

MAKE THE HOT FUDGE SAUCE

10 In a medium saucepan, combine the cream, butter, brown sugar, sugar, and salt with a whisk. Bring to a simmer for about a minute.

11 Remove from the heat, add the chocolate chips, and whisk until the mixture is smooth.

12 Add the cocoa powder and whisk until all the lumps are gone.

13 Return the pan to the heat and whisk over medium-low heat for another 30 seconds, then remove from the heat and add the vanilla.

14 Set the pan aside on a heat-safe surface, but leave the hot fudge in the pan.

MAKE THE STRAWBERRY WHIPPED CREAM

15 In the bowl of a stand mixer with the paddle attachment, stir the cream cheese, salt, and sugar together.

16 Add the strawberry powder and mix on low speed until the cream cheese is light pink.

17 Add the heavy cream and whisk on medium with the whisk attachment until stiff peaks form.

MAKE THE GANACHE

18 Using a knife and chopping board, chop the chocolate, put it into a medium bowl, and set aside.

19 Pour the cream into a small saucepan and, over medium-high heat, bring the cream to a boil.

20 Turn off the heat and pour the cream over the chocolate. Cover the bowl with a kitchen towel and let it sit for 3 minutes.

21 Remove the towel and whisk the ganache till it's shiny.

22 Cover with the towel again and set aside.

TO ASSEMBLE THE SUNDAES

23 Line 2 sheet pans with parchment paper.

24 Cut each profiterole in half so you get a top and a bottom.

25 Organize all the bottoms on one prepared sheet pan.

26 Stir the ganache, dip each top into the ganache, and then place them on a separate prepared sheet pan.

27 Put the pan of tops in the fridge for a few minutes to let the chocolate set.

28 Line up 8 big bowls, or enough for as many servings as you need.

29 Heat the hot fudge over the stove for a few seconds and spoon a few tablespoons into each bowl.

30 Place 3 or 4 profiterole bottoms into the bowls.

31 Using a scoop that is about the same size as a finished profiterole, scoop vanilla ice cream onto each profiterole bottom.

32 Place a ganache-dipped top onto each of the scoops of ice cream.

33 Spoon a few tablespoons of strawberry whipped cream onto each profiterole.

34 Garnish each profiterole with a maraschino cherry.

THE SCIENCE OF PÂTE À CHOUX

The science of pâte à choux is really cool. Pâte à choux puffs up in the oven when you bake it. There are a few different things that make this happen. First, when you are cooking the dough, you mix the flour, butter, and water really hard. This stretches out all the protein in the flour and makes it like a microscopic net. The water also hydrates the starch in the flour and turns it into a sticky goo. You mix eggs into the cooked flour, and this introduces a different protein to the net, adds fat to the recipe so it tastes good, and adds even more water to the dough. When you pipe out shapes with the pâte à choux and put it in the oven, lots of cool things happen. First, the sticky goo made from the hydrated flour creates a coating around the protein net and, when the goo gets hot, it gelatinizes, or basically gets stretchy like a balloon. Next, all the water starts to turn to steam. Since steam takes up much more space than water, the steam makes the pâte à choux expand. The stretchy outside layer keeps the protein net from exploding as it expands, and then eventually all the water is cooked out. When that happens, the stretchy layer gets hard and crispy, and that's when you have a delicious choux puff. Crispy on the outside, hollow in the middle. Fascinating, right?

RAINBOW ÉCLAIRS

MAKES 24 4-inch éclairs

One of the fun things you can make with pâte à choux is an éclair. It kinda looks like a hot dog bun, but instead of cutting it open and putting a sausage in it, you poke holes in it, fill it with cream, and dip it in chocolate. I do love éclairs, but I'm not sure I love them more than hot dogs. Hot dogs are sandwiches, but are they also some kind of pastry? Anyway, éclairs are also fun to eat because sometimes the filling shoots out the side, and you try to catch it, not because you're trying to avoid it hitting your shirt, but because you don't want to waste any of the delicious cream.

PREP TIME 45 minutes
BAKING TIME 22 to 27 minutes

Ingredients

FOR THE ÉCLAIRS
1 recipe pâte à choux (page 45)

FOR THE DIPLOMAT CREAM
4 large (56 grams) egg yolks

½ cup (100 grams) granulated sugar

3 tablespoons (30 grams) cornstarch

2 cups (480 grams) whole milk

Pinch of kosher salt

2 teaspoons (10 grams) pure vanilla extract

2 tablespoons (28 grams) unsalted butter, room temperature

1½ cups (341 grams) heavy cream

FOR THE GLAZE
1½ cups (250 grams) white chocolate chips

3½ cups (400 grams) fondant icing sugar (if you can't find it, use powdered sugar)

2 to 3 tablespoons water, plus more to loosen

3 food coloring colors, whichever you like!

EQUIPMENT

- Parchment paper
- 2 sheet pans
- Medium or large French star piping tip
- 4 piping bags
- Small piping tip
- Medium bowl
- Whisk
- Medium saucepan
- Plastic wrap
- Stand mixer
- Rubber spatula
- 5 small bowls
- 3 medium small plain tips
- Small saucepan
- Pencil

RECIPE CONTINUES

MAKE THE ÉCLAIR PASTRY

1 Preheat the oven to 400°F.

2 Draw 4-inch-long lines, parallel to each other, approximately 4 inches apart, on a piece of parchment paper that will fit on a sheet pan.

3 Flip the paper over and place it on a sheet pan.

4 Using a medium to large French star piping tip, fill a piping bag with the choux dough. Pipe out even lines of pâte à choux over the lines you drew.

5 Bake the éclair pastries for 10 to 12 minutes.

6 Turn the heat down to 350°F and bake for another 12 to 15 minutes, or until the éclairs are golden brown and feel crispy on the outside and sound hollow inside when they're tapped.

7 Remove the pan from the oven.

8 Holding a clean kitchen towel, pick up each éclair and, using a small piping tip, poke 3 holes in a line on the bottom of the éclairs to allow the steam to escape, and then set them aside to cool completely.

MAKE THE DIPLOMAT CREAM

9 In a medium bowl, whisk together the yolks and ¼ cup of the sugar until lighter in color.

10 Add the cornstarch, whisk, and set aside.

11 In a medium saucepan over medium heat, heat up the milk, remaining ¼ cup sugar, and salt until it almost boils.

12 Put the bowl of egg mixture on a damp kitchen towel.

13 With one hand, whisk the egg mixture. With the other hand, slowly drizzle in the hot milk. Keep whisking the whole time.

14 Pour the pastry cream back into the saucepan and cook, keep stirring, on medium-high heat until the mixture is thick and one bubble plops up on top.

15 Remove the pastry cream from the heat and pour it back into a medium bowl. Don't scrape the bottom of the pot unless it's clean. If it is burned or looks like scrambled eggs, leave it in there to be cleaned up.

16 Stir in the butter and vanilla until the butter melts.

17 Place a piece of plastic wrap over the bowl and refrigerate for at least 2 hours until it's cool.

18 When the pastry cream is cool, return it to the bowl of a stand mixer with the paddle attachment and whip it on medium speed until the cream is light and fluffy.

19 Using a rubber spatula, put the pastry cream in a small bowl and set aside.

RECIPE CONTINUES

PÂTE À CHOUX 52

20 Add the heavy cream to the mixing bowl and whip until soft peaks form, about 4 minutes.

21 With the rubber spatula, put a little of the whipped cream into the pastry cream and fold it a few times. Add the remaining whipped cream and gently fold a few more times. It's okay if it's not completely folded. It gets folded one more time later.

22 Line up the éclairs on a parchment-lined sheet pan. Pipe some diplomat cream into each hole of each éclair.

23 Place the filled éclairs into the fridge.

MAKE THE GLAZE

24 Get out 5 small bowls and a small saucepan. The saucepan needs to be smaller than the bowl.

25 Fill the saucepan with a few inches of water and set it to simmer on low heat.

26 Fill one bowl with the white chocolate.

27 In the other bowl, whisk together the powdered sugar and water.

28 Place the bowl of white chocolate over the simmering water and let it sit for 2 minutes to melt the chocolate. Don't burn yourself on the steam coming out the sides!

29 Gently whisk the chocolate a few times and then remove from the heat and set aside. Keep the heat on.

30 Next, heat up the sugar-water mixture by whisking it over the simmering water.

31 Pour the hot sugar mixture into the melted white chocolate and whisk until all the lumps are gone.

32 Then divide the glaze into 3 small bowls. Add whichever colors you'd like to each bowl and stir to combine. You can either pour the colors in their own cornets or small piping bag, or you can keep them in their bowls and use spoons to drizzle.

FINISH THE ÉCLAIRS

33 Get the cream-filled éclair pastries out of the fridge.

34 Cover 2 sheet pans with a clean sheet of parchment.

35 Drizzle one color on the éclairs. Quickly, repeat with the other two colors until they look psychedelic and cool. If your glaze starts to thicken too much, just add a little more water, or reheat it over the double boiler to loosen it.

36 Once the éclairs have each color, take them off the tray and place on the clean baking sheet so the glaze "legs" don't break off.

Duff's Tip

Éclairs don't keep very long. Try to serve and eat them within a few hours of making them. I know it's tough, but try to eat them all.

DEEP-FRYING
SAFETY TIPS

Deep-frying food can make it really delicious and crispy, but deep-frying can be super dangerous, and you have to be wicked careful when you do it. Here are some tips:

1 **Always have an adult help you.** Always. Don't even think about deep-frying alone. You could be burned really badly or even start a fire.

2 **Never overfill the pot you are frying in.** Make sure there is plenty of space between the surface of the oil and the top edge of the pot.

3 **Never put water or anything else wet into hot oil.** It'll immediately turn to steam violently and can cause burns and fires. Always make sure your pot is completely dry before adding oil to it.

4 **Keep any long pan handles turned into the center of the stove,** never sticking out where someone could walk by and knock the pot off the stove.

5 **Make sure the oil you are using has a high smoke point,** like vegetable oil or peanut oil. Olive oil has a very low smoke point and is no good for deep-frying.

6 **Get the kind of thermometer that clips to the side of the pot** and stays in the oil the entire time, so you can keep the oil temperature steady.

7 **Keep the lid of the pot handy.** If the oil starts to bubble over or catches on fire, having the lid nearby will allow you to quickly smother any uncontrolled event.

8 **Let the oil cool** before trying to dispose of it.

9 **Don't pour oil down the drain.** When the oil cools it can clog your pipes. Pour the cooled oil into an old milk container or something like that.

10 **If there is a fire, NEVER use water to put it out.** Water makes the fire much worse. Know where the fire extinguisher is, and if you don't have one (get one), you can use flour or baking soda.

11 **Don't try to fry everything at once.** A crowded fryer can boil over. Always fry in smaller batches.

12 **Be safe** and make delicious stuff!

CHURROS

MAKES

25

churros

The first time I ever had a churro was in the town of Valladolid in Mexico. My friends and I had been swimming in a cenote and we were super hungry. I saw this guy with a cart and he was frying something. And fried things usually taste good when you're hungry. I didn't know what I was ordering, but I got a bunch of long, skinny fried pastries rolled in cinnamon sugar and served in a newspaper cone, and they were quite possibly one of the most delicious things I've ever tasted.

PREP TIME
20 minutes
COOKING TIME
1 to 2 minutes
per churro

Ingredients

1 cup plus 2 tablespoons (266 grams) water

3 tablespoons (48 grams) granulated sugar

¼ teaspoon (2 grams) kosher salt

¼ cup (54 grams) vegetable oil, plus 2 quarts, for frying

1 cup (150 grams) all-purpose flour

FOR THE CINNAMON SUGAR

½ cup granulated sugar

2 teaspoons ground cinnamon

EQUIPMENT

- Small saucepan
- Wide-bottomed dish
- Wooden spoon
- Medium bowl
- Sheet pan
- Paper towels or a wire rack
- Candy thermometer
- Tall pot
- Piping bag
- Large star tip
- Kitchen scissors
- Slotted spoon, metal tongs, or spider

RECIPE CONTINUES

1 In a small saucepan over medium heat, cook the water, sugar, salt, and ¼ cup of vegetable oil until you see the first bubble.

2 Remove from the heat, add the flour, and mix with a wooden spoon until the dough forms a ball.

3 Cover the saucepan and let it cool a bit.

4 Line a sheet pan with paper towels or a wire rack.

5 Clip a candy thermometer to the side of a tall pot over medium-high heat, make a deep fryer by bringing 2 quarts of oil to 375°F. (Be very careful. Oil can spatter!)

6 Put the churro dough into a piping bag with a large star tip. Pipe 5 3-inch-long logs directly into the oil, using a pair of cooking scissors to trim the log when it's long enough. Fry 5 at a time so you don't overcrowd the oil. Don't worry if they're not all exactly the same.

7 In a wide-bottomed dish, combine the sugar and ground cinnamon. Set aside.

8 Fry the churros until they're golden and, using a slotted spoon or spider, remove them from the oil.

9 Drain them on paper towels on the prepared sheet pan.

10 Sprinkle cinnamon sugar over the churros while they're still hot. Repeat until all the churros have been fried and sugar coated. And don't forget to turn off the heat.

11 Eat immediately.

Duff's Tip

I like to dip my churros in ganache, dulce de leche, Nutella, jam, butterscotch, or honey.

CHAPTER

3

DONUTS

CAKE DONUT
BREAD PUDDING

Okay, I know this never happens but, just for fun, let's say you have cake donuts sitting around that have gone stale. Impossible, I know, but let's just imagine it happened. You don't want to throw them away; that would be a waste. So, you really only have one option: Make bread pudding. It's really best when you serve it with cold ice cream on top. And caramel sauce. Oh, and chocolate chips. It's called "bread pudding" because originally it was made with stale bread, which might sound gross, but if you have old (but not too old!) bread sitting around, try this recipe with it. You'll freak out it's so good.

MAKES
1
9 × 13-inch pan

PREP TIME
10 minutes
BAKING TIME
35 to 45 minutes

Ingredients

1¼ cups (250 grams) granulated sugar

Pinch of kosher salt

7 large eggs

3 cups (480 grams) whole milk

1 tablespoon (14 grams) pure vanilla extract

10 to 12 cake donuts, cut into ¾-inch cubes, arranged on a sheet pan, and either dried overnight, uncovered, or baked at 350°F for 10 minutes

½ cup (93 grams) lightly packed light brown sugar

¼ cup (½ stick or 57 grams) unsalted butter, softened

EQUIPMENT

- 9 × 13-inch baking dish
- Cooking spray
- 2 medium bowls
- Whisk
- Kitchen towel
- Wooden spoon

RECIPE CONTINUES

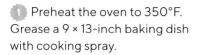

1. Preheat the oven to 350°F. Grease a 9 × 13-inch baking dish with cooking spray.

2. In a medium bowl, whisk together the granulated sugar, salt, eggs, milk, and vanilla in a bowl until the sugar is mostly dissolved and it's all the same light yellow color.

3. Put the donut pieces in the prepared baking dish and pour the custard mixture over them. Gently press down a few times to make sure all the donut pieces are wet with custard. Cover with a kitchen towel and let sit for 10 minutes at room temperature.

4. In another bowl using a wooden spoon, mix together the soft butter, brown sugar, and a pinch of salt. If the mixture is loose, add more brown sugar until it gets crumbly. Sprinkle the top of the bread pudding with the sugar mixture.

5. Bake for 35 to 45 minutes, or just until the bread pudding is only slightly jiggly in the center. To test, using an oven mitt, carefully grab the oven rack and give it a little shake. If the middle sloshes around, it's not done. If it it gives a firm jiggle, it's done.

6. Cover and let it cool in the fridge before serving.

Duff's Tip

This dish reheats very well. Keep it in the fridge, covered, for up to 3 days.

WHAT IS A CUSTARD?

When you're making desserts, sometimes you hear the word custard. There are all kinds of custards, and you can find them in lots of different desserts. Custards are basically any mixture of eggs, cream, and flavorings. Custards are always cooked really slow so they are smooth and velvety. There are many different kinds of custards, including crème brûlée, pastry cream, pudding, flan, cheesecake, crème anglaise, and ice cream. I like the sound of the word custard. It just sounds delicious.

DONUTS

Don't be scared. Yeast isn't scary. Deep-frying isn't scary (if you follow the Deep-Frying Tips on page 56). Knowing how to make yeast donuts from scratch basically makes you a wizard. Learning how to deep-fry means you can make your own French fries. Learning how to work with yeast means you can make your own burger buns. Learn how to raise a cow and you can have a barbecue from scratch.

Ingredients

FOR THE DONUTS

1 cup plus 2 tablespoons (114 grams) granulated sugar

2 packets (14 grams) active dry yeast

1¼ cups (300 grams) warm water (do not exceed 119°F)

6 cups plus 2 teaspoons (908 grams) bread flour, plus more for dusting

2 large eggs

½ cup plus 2 tablespoons (114 grams) vegetable shortening, at room temperature

1¼ cups (282 grams) buttermilk, at room temperature

½ teaspoon (3 grams) kosher salt

FOR THE FILLING

½ cup (100 grams) granulated sugar

¼ cup (35 grams) cornstarch

Pinch of kosher salt

2 cups (480 grams) whole milk

4 large (56 grams) egg yolks

1 teaspoon (5 grams) pure vanilla extract

FOR THE GLAZE

3 cups (360 grams) powdered sugar

½ cup (50 grams) cocoa powder

6 to 8 tablespoons (90 to 120 grams) whole milk

2 teaspoons (10 grams) pure vanilla extract

2 quarts vegetable oil, for frying

EQUIPMENT

- Stand mixer
- Candy thermometer
- Rubber spatula
- 2 medium bowls
- Plastic wrap
- Rolling pin
- Biscuit cutter or donut cutter
- 2 sheet pans
- Tall pot

- 2 wire racks
- Tongs, wooden chopsticks, or spider
- Whisk
- Medium saucepan
- Bismarck tip
- Piping bag
- Kitchen towel

RECIPE CONTINUES

MAKE THE DONUTS

1 In the bowl of a stand mixer with no attachment (for now), mix the sugar, yeast, and warm water with a rubber spatula. Using a candy thermometer, make sure the water is not too hot (do not exceed 119°F) or the yeast will die. Let the yeast bloom for 7 minutes. The water will get foamy.

2 Add the flour, eggs, shortening, and buttermilk, and with the dough-hook attachment, mix the dough on slow speed for 4 minutes. (The dough might climb the hook now and then. Just turn off the mixer and push it back down with a rubber spatula.)

3 Increase the speed to medium and mix for about 15 minutes or until the dough is smooth, shiny, and a little sticky.

4 Add the salt and mix for 1 more minute.

5 Remove the dough-hook attachment from the mixer bowl, and then move the dough to a lightly oiled medium bowl.

6 Cover the dough with plastic wrap and let it rise until it is pushing against the plastic wrap.

7 Remove the plastic wrap, punch down the dough so it deflates, and then repeat to let it rise again. This should take about 2 hours.

8 Turn the dough out onto a flour-dusted surface. Sprinkle some flour onto two sheet pans.

9 Using a rolling pin, roll out the dough until it's about ¾ inch thick.

10 Using a biscuit cutter, cut the dough in circles (or if you have a donut cutter, cut it into rings).

11 Place the shaped dough onto the prepared sheet pans, dust the tops of the donuts with flour, and carefully and loosely cover with plastic wrap.

12 Let the donuts rise for 20 to 25 minutes.

13 Put 3 inches of oil in a tall pot and clip a candy thermometer to the side of the pot so that the bulb is immersed in the oil. Candy thermometers can go to really high temperatures and are usually nice and long and safe for deep-frying.

14 Fit a wire rack onto a sheet pan.

15 Heat the oil to 375°F and fry the donuts in batches, until they are brown on one side, then carefully flip them using tongs or wooden chopsticks. There should be a white line around the middle of the donuts when they're done. It should take about a minute and a half per side.

16 Remove the donuts with tongs (gently!) or a spider (a spider is like a screen with a long handle) and let the donuts cool on the wire rack.

MAKE THE FILLING

17 Mix the sugar, cornstarch, salt, milk, yolks, and vanilla in a medium bowl with a wire whisk.

18 Pour everything into a medium saucepan and cook on medium heat until the mixture is thick.

19 Pour the mixture back into the bowl, cover with plastic wrap so the plastic is touching the filling, and cool in the fridge for about 30 to 45 minutes.

MAKE THE CHOCOLATE GLAZE

20 In a medium bowl, whisk together the powdered sugar and cocoa powder to get all the lumps out.

21 Add 4 tablespoons of milk and the vanilla, whisking until smooth.

22 Add another tablespoon of milk and whisk again. (If it looks dippable, stop. If it's too thick, add 1 more tablespoon of milk.)

23 Cover the bowl with a kitchen towel and keep at room temperature until you are ready to use it.

TO ASSEMBLE THE DONUTS

24 Whisk the cooled filling either by hand or in the bowl of a stand mixer with the whisk attachment.

25 Fit a Bismarck tip onto a piping bag and, using a rubber spatula, add the filling to the piping bag, twisting the back of the bag and tying it off with a twist tie.

26 Stick the Bismarck tip into the donut somewhere along the white line and squeeze gently until you feel the donut get heavier. Repeat with all the donuts.

TO GLAZE THE DONUTS

27 Dip each donut top into the chocolate glaze, using the edge of the bowl to remove excess glaze. (Note: If you wanna add sprinkles, do it now, before the glaze hardens!)

28 Let the glaze harden at room temperature for about 20 minutes on a sheet pan lined with parchment.

29 *Kaboom*, you made Wicked-Good Boston Cream Donuts. Nice job.

Duff's Tip

If you made classic ring donuts, dip the donuts but don't fill them. There's a hole in the middle. Duh.

DONUTS
FROM AROUND THE WORLD

BEIGNETS
NEW ORLEANS

Square donuts are covered with LOTS of powdered sugar.

MALASADAS
PORTUGAL

One of my favorite donuts. Light and fluffy and crispy, rolled in granulated sugar and filled with cream. One time I had a malasada in Hawaii, and it was filled with barbecued pork!

CHURROS
MEXICO

These are basically deep-fried pâte à choux. Traditionally dusted with cinnamon sugar, they are now filled with Nutella or jam, dunked in syrup, and even piped into crazy shapes.

BUÑUELOS
SOUTH AMERICA

Little dough balls are fried, rolled in cinnamon sugar, and served with honey. Eat these for good luck.

OLIEBOLLEN
BELGIUM

Belgium is really good at frying stuff. (Belgian fries are the best anywhere.) These donuts are big balls of sweet, fried dough rolled in powdered sugar. At Christmastime, they put raisins and nuts in them.

YOUTIAO
CHINA

One of my favorite street foods. They're really long and not sweet, but they're really crispy and delicious when dunked in syrup.

BERLINERS
GERMANY

This type of fried dough is usually filled with jam or marmalade but can also be filled with cream or custard.

SUFGANIYOT
ISRAEL

These jam-filled donuts are denser than American donuts and the ratio of jelly to dough is almost one to one.

AN
JAPAN

This thin, light fried dough is filled with slightly sweet red bean paste.

SFENJ
NORTH AFRICA

These guys are super crispy and not very sweet. They're great when dipped in honey, jam, or syrup.

Donuts are one of the greatest foods ever. Almost every country in the world has some kind of donut. When you are traveling, eating the local food is one of the best ways to get to know another culture, so as you travel the world, remember to eat a donut in every place you visit.

· DONUT-FLAVORED ·
PLASTIC BAG
ICE CREAM

MAKES ABOUT 2 cups

Making ice cream is really fun.
Making ice cream with your friends while
playing catch is *super* fun.

PREP TIME
10 minutes
"CHURNING" TIME
7 minutes

Ingredients

1 cup (230 grams) whole milk

1 cup (240 grams) half-and-half

2 tablespoons (25 grams) granulated sugar

½ teaspoon (2 grams) pure vanilla extract

Pinch of kosher salt

1 donut, any flavor, chopped up into little pieces and dried overnight, or baked at 350°F for 10 minutes

3 pounds of ice cubes

½ cup (113 grams) rock salt for making ice cream

EQUIPMENT

• Large bowl

• Whisk

• Quart resealable plastic bag

• Gallon resealable plastic bag

• A friend

RECIPE CONTINUES

1 In a large bowl, whisk together the milk, half-and-half, sugar, vanilla, and salt.

2 In a quart resealable plastic bag, put the donut pieces in the milk mixture. Be sure the bag is tightly sealed, but leave a little air in there so the ice cream has room to expand.

3 Put half (about 1 ½ pounds) of the ice cubes, or enough to fill your bag halfway, and half of the rock salt in the bottom of a gallon resealable plastic bag.

4 Place the quart bag inside the gallon bag and then add in the rest of the ice cubes and rock salt. (Make sure the quart bag has ice all around it and if you can fit a little more ice, go for it—but make sure the bag can close easily.)

5 Play catch with your friend for about 7 minutes with the bag. You can also put a towel on your counter and roll the bag around on top of it. If it isn't as firm as you'd like it, stick it in the freezer for 20-30 minutes until it is.

6 Abracadabra! Ice cream for you and your friend!

Note

It won't be as firm as the ice cream you buy at the store, but it'll be nice and creamy.

THE SCIENCE OF ICE CREAM

Ice cream sounds simple. Put some sugar in some cream and freeze it, right? Not exactly. Ice cream is delicious not only because of the yummy stuff you put in it but also because of the texture. The texture of ice cream is smooth and, well, creamy. Here's how and why that is: For one thing, lots of ice creams are made with egg yolks that, when cooked very slowly with the sugar and the milk, make a custard. A custard-based ice cream, or frozen custard, will be thicker and richer than ice cream made with only milk. Next, *how* the ice cream is frozen contributes to making it creamy and not grainy. If you just put the ice-cream liquid in the freezer, you'll get one big block of ice cream, because ice is a crystal and the ice cream will freeze as one big crystal. Ice-cream machines spin so that, as the ice cream freezes, the ice crystals stay really, really small. So small that they can fit *in between* your taste buds so you don't even know that they're there. Ice cream that feels grainy is ice cream that wasn't moving fast enough as it froze. Sometimes ice cream can be greasy in your mouth. This happens when the ice cream is churned too much and the fat from the cream and the eggs separates into clumps. It's important to spin ice cream at just the right speed. Once you get a perfect, smooth ice cream, now you have to freeze it again. Churned ice cream is put into a container and then placed in the freezer so it can harden up and also preserve that creamy texture.

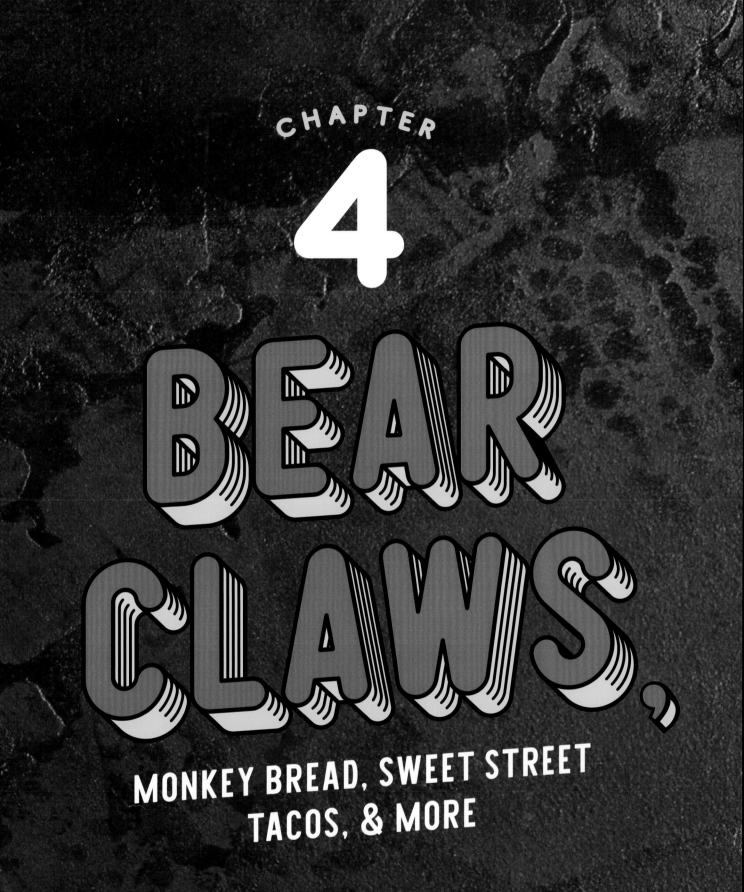

CHAPTER

4

BEAR CLAWS,

MONKEY BREAD, SWEET STREET TACOS, & MORE

A BRIEF HISTORY OF BAKING

People have been baking stuff for a long time. The oldest oven ever discovered was from almost 7,000 years ago. Ancient Egyptians were the first people known to bake bread with yeast. They had mastered yeast by brewing beer, which is basically just liquid bread. The knowledge of yeast traveled to ancient Greece, where they invented enclosed ovens instead of baking over coals or hot stones. Ovens dating back to 5600 BC can be found in the Middle East, including Turkey and Israel. In 300 BC in ancient Rome, baking really took off. Romans loved baking so much that pastry chefs, known as *pastillaria*, were celebrities! Imagine that.

But then Rome got clobbered by the Ostrogoths and the Visigoths and the Vandals and the Gauls and the Franks and all the other barbarians. All that clobbering set things back a bit in the baking world (not to mention science, art, government, medicine, architecture, engineering, etc.), and Europe entered a period called the Dark Ages. Not many people had ovens back then, and most baking was done by one family for a whole community. Only wealthy people could afford an oven, or even wheat flour for that matter.

Poor people ate mostly dark breads like rye that was coarsely milled. Rich people had white breads, cakes, and pies made with finely milled, expensive flour made from wheat. This is where the term *upper crust* comes from to describe rich people. After about 1,000 years of pretty boring breads and pastries, things started to get interesting again. People were traveling all over the world and sharing exotic grains and spices and sugar, and bakers had more ingredients to make better stuff, like wiggs, which were small buns made with a sweet dough filled with spices and herbs, and mince pies, which were (and still are) stuffed with chopped, spiced beef or lamb. Around 1500, gingerbread started showing up, although nobody knows who made the first gingerbread house. After this period, more people had enough money to buy ovens and ingredients. Sugar became much cheaper because it was much easier to get and people began baking all sorts of pies and cakes. Mincemeat pies were now filled with sweet, dried fruit and exotic spices, and more people were baking yeast cakes closer to what you and I think of as cake today. Around this time, cookbooks became much more widespread and recipes could be shared more widely.

In the 1700s, bakers started getting better equipment and things like "cake hoops" were invented. These were the first standard cake pans and were lined with buttered paper. Soon after that, schools for baking began to appear in London. People could go and learn all sorts of baking and pastry-making techniques. Being a good baker was finally cool again!

In the 1800s, chemical leaveners like baking soda and baking powder started becoming available to everyone, and baking really took off. All kinds of pastries were available to home bakers that didn't involve using yeast or complicated classic French techniques to make things rise. Pancakes, muffins, cakes, quick breads, biscuits, and other kinds of pastries were now enjoyed widely. The industrial revolution made quality ovens much more inexpensive and more and more people were able to bake more in their own homes.

During the 1900s, it became commonplace for *everyone* to have a birthday cake, which made children all over the world really excited. And in 2002, a baker named Duff opened a little cake shop in Baltimore, Maryland, called Charm City Cakes. He started making cakes that looked like things other than cakes, but the results tasted amazing, and cake decorating has never been the same.

A rare Charm City Cake that looks like a regular cake.

BEAR CLAWS

Bear claws rule. The dough is really flaky and buttery. The filling is made with almonds and has the coolest texture. It's velvety but firm—like a candy. I like taking 2 days to make this recipe. I make the dough and the filling first, and then I let the dough rest overnight in the fridge. Resting the dough overnight allows the gluten to relax, so that when I bake it, it doesn't shrink.

PREP TIME
2 hours, plus 3 or more hours for resting

BAKING TIME
20 to 22 minutes

Ingredients

FOR THE PASTRY

3½ cups (525 grams) all-purpose flour, refrigerated, plus more for dusting

1½ cups (3 sticks or 339 grams) cold unsalted butter

½ cup (118 grams) warm water (do not exceed 119°F)

¼ cup (50 grams) granulated sugar

2 packages (14 grams) active dry yeast

2 large eggs, at room temperature

½ cup (135 grams) half-and-half

Pinch of kosher salt

FOR THE FILLING

8 ounces (227 grams) almond paste

1 large (40 grams) egg white

¾ cup (90 grams) powdered sugar

1 teaspoon (4 grams) ground cinnamon

Pinch of salt

FOR THE TOPPING

1 large egg

Pinch of kosher salt

Pinch of sugar

Sliced almonds

Powdered sugar, for dusting

EQUIPMENT

- Food processor
- Chef's knife
- Large bowl
- Wooden spoon
- Kitchen towel
- Medium bowl
- Whisk
- Plastic wrap
- Stand mixer
- Rolling pin
- Parchment paper
- Sheet pan
- Small bowl
- Pastry brush
- Wire rack

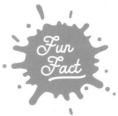

Fun Fact

When you make bear claws in a professional bakery, the filling of the new bear claws is made with the ground up bear claws from yesterday.

RECIPE CONTINUES

MAKE THE DOUGH

Part 1

1. Put the flour in the bowl of a food processor with a blade attachment.

2. Using a chef's knife, slice the cold butter into pats. Add them to the flour.

3. In a large bowl, mix the ingredients with a wooden spoon, so all the pats of butter separate from each other and get coated in flour.

4. Pulse the food processor until the butter looks like little pebbles.

5. Take the flour-butter mixture out of the food processor, put it back in the large bowl, cover with a kitchen towel, and put the bowl in the fridge.

Part 2

6. In a medium bowl, whisk the warm water with a pinch of the sugar.

7. Stir in the yeast until it dissolves, and then cover the bowl with a kitchen towel.

8. In 7 minutes, check the yeast mixture. It should be foamy and tan and smell amazing.

9. Add the eggs, half-and-half, sugar, and salt into the yeast. Whisk so everything gets mixed together well, especially the eggs.

10. Let the mixture sit for about 15 minutes to cool.

Part 3

11. This next step you gotta do kinda fast.

12. Take the flour mixture out of the fridge. Dump the yeast mixture into the flour mixture.

13. With a wooden spoon, stir it around until all the flour is wet.

14. Cover the bowl with plastic wrap and refrigerate until you're ready. If you have to finish this recipe today, wait at least 3 hours before taking the dough out of the fridge. If you can wait until tomorrow, do so.

MAKE THE FILLING

15. In the bowl of a stand mixer with the paddle attachment, beat together the almond paste, egg white, powdered sugar, cinnamon, and salt until smooth.

16. Cover the bowl with plastic wrap and refrigerate until you're ready to fill the bear claws.

MAKE THE PASTRIES

17. Remove the dough from the fridge and turn it out on a lightly floured surface. With your hands, form the dough into a rough square.

18. Dust the top with flour and, using a rolling pin, roll the dough out until it is about 18 inches × 16 inches.

19. Fold the dough into thirds and place it in the fridge for 15 minutes.

20. Repeat: Roll out, fold, fridge.

21. Roll the dough out again, to 18 inches × 16 inches and then cut it lengthwise into four long strips that are 4 inches wide. Work with 1 strip at a time, putting the rest of the strips in the fridge while you work.

22. Spread 2 tablespoons of the almond-paste filling down the center of one of the strips.

23. Roll the strip up from the long side so dough overlaps the seam.

24. Place the strip seam side down and then cut it into 5 equal pieces. Gently, slightly flatten each piece with your hand.

25 Using a chef's knife, cut 3 or 4 slits for the bear toes, place the bear claw on a parchment-covered sheet pan, and curve the bear claw so the toes spread out.

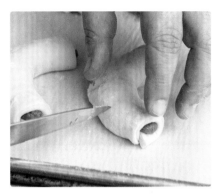

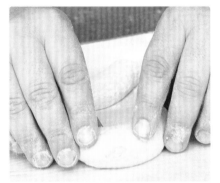

26 In a small bowl, make an egg wash with the egg, salt and sugar.

27 Using a pastry brush, brush each bear claw with egg wash, sprinkle with sliced almonds. Repeat with the remaining strips. Cover with plastic loosely and let the bear claws rise for 30 minutes or until they are poofy.

28 Heat the oven to 400°F. Bake the bear claws for 20 to 22 minutes, depending on how big the bear claw is. The bigger the bear claw, the longer it will take to bake. When they're fully baked, they'll be nice and golden brown on top and flaky inside. And they'll smell heavenly.

29 Carefully remove the bear claws from the oven. Allow the bear claws to cool on a wire rack.

30 When they are completely cool, dust with powdered sugar and serve.

Note

My favorite thing about bear claws is taking one in each hand, pretending I'm a real bear. Seriously. I growl and eat salmon and do other bear stuff whenever I make bear claws.

MONKEY BREAD

MAKES

1

monkey loaf, or
12 servings

Monkey bread got its name because you pull it
apart and eat it like a monkey. I always make monkey noises
when I eat monkey bread. But I don't throw poo at
anyone. If you don't wanna make the dough from scratch,
you can use store-bought biscuit mix.

PREP TIME
30 minutes, plus
2 hours for rising

BAKING TIME
30 to 40
minutes

Ingredients

FOR THE DOUGH

1¼ cups (335 grams) warm milk

1 package (7 grams) active dry yeast

¼ cup (50 grams) granulated sugar

1 large egg

¼ cup (½ stick or 57 grams) unsalted
butter, melted

Pinch of kosher salt

4 cups (600 grams) all-purpose
flour

FOR THE SAUCE

1 cup (2 sticks or 226 grams)
unsalted butter, melted

1 cup (185 grams) lightly packed
light brown sugar

Pinch of kosher salt

1 tablespoon (12 grams) ground
cinnamon

EQUIPMENT

- **Stand mixer**
- **Whisk**
- **Kitchen towel**
- **Medium saucepan**
- **Sheet pan**
- **Standard (10-cup) Bundt pan**

 RECIPE CONTINUES

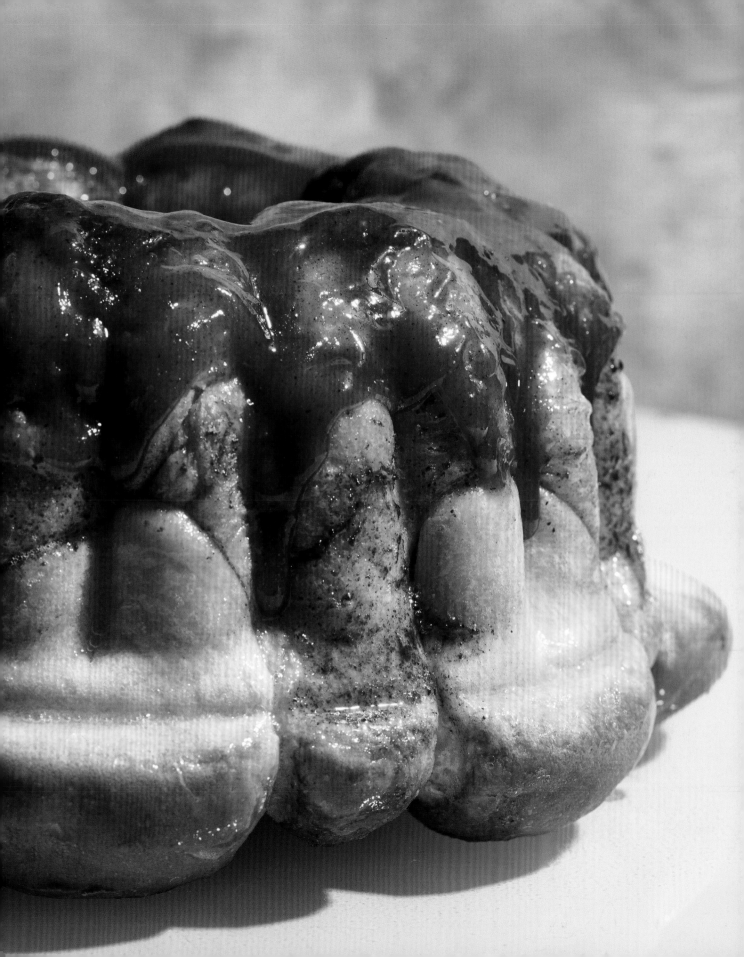

MAKE THE DOUGH

1 In the bowl of a stand mixer, mix the warm milk and the yeast.

2 Cover with a towel and let the yeast bloom and get foamy for about 7 minutes.

3 Add the sugar, egg, melted butter, and salt and whisk together so everything is smooth.

4 Add the flour to the mixture and, using the dough hook on medium speed for 5 minutes, mix until the dough is a smooth ball.

5 Remove the bowl from the mixer, cover with a kitchen towel, and let the dough rise for an hour in a warm spot (like on top of the fridge).

6 Punch the dough down and let it rise again, in the same bowl, for another hour.

MAKE THE CINNAMON SAUCE

7 In a medium saucepan over medium-high heat, melt the butter. Then whisk in the brown sugar, salt, and cinnamon. Whisking the entire time, heat the mixture until it's just about to bubble.

8 Set aside to cool.

TO BAKE THE BREAD

9 Place an oven rack on the lowest rung in the oven and a second rack on the middle rung. Put a sheet pan on the lowest rack to catch anything that drips.

10 Preheat the oven to 375°F.

11 Remove the dough from the bowl and place on a clean, lightly floured surface.

12 Roll out the dough and then cut it into 1-inch-wide strips. Then cut the strips into squares.

13 Using your hands, roll the dough into 1-inch balls. You'll have a lot of balls.

14 Grease the Bundt pan as shown with vegetable oil spray.

15 Pour some of the sauce into the Bundt pan.

16 Layer about half the dough balls into the pan.

17 Pour half of the cinnamon sauce that you have left over the dough balls.

18 Layer in the rest of the dough balls.

19 Pour the remaining sauce over the dough balls in the pan.

20 Cover the pan with plastic wrap and let rest for 30 minutes.

21 Place the monkey bread in the oven.

22 Bake for 30 to 40 minutes, or until the top is a rich, golden brown.

23 Carefully remove from the oven and let the monkey bread rest for 5 minutes before turning it out onto a plate.

THE SCIENCE OF YEAST

Yeast is the stuff that makes bread rise. But how? Yeast is a single-celled fungus, like a really small mushroom. It's so small that it takes 20,000,000,000 yeast cells to make 1 gram of yeast. Basically what happens is that yeast eats sugar and, as it turns out, the starch in flour is a sugar. So when you mix yeast with water and flour, the yeast cells feed on the starch in the dough and then turn it into ethanol and carbon dioxide. The carbon dioxide and ethanol get trapped in the dough by the protein in the flour, called gluten. The dough rises because the carbon dioxide has nowhere to go, so it expands in the dough. When you bake the bread, the carbon dioxide expands even more and the ethanol turns to steam, and the steam helps the bread rise, too (and it makes the bread taste good). Yeast also help break down proteins that help turn the gluten into a big net to trap all that stuff. So when you are baking bread, you are baking with something ALIVE!

• L.A. STREET DESSERT •

TACOS

MAKES
20
small tacos

Street tacos in Los Angeles are one of my favorite things to eat. Usually, small flour tortillas are filled with pretty much any kind of meat (I like chorizo) and then whatever else I want. There's different sauces, vegetables, pickles, hot peppers...pretty much whatever you can stomach. These dessert tacos are the same idea, but instead of using flour tortillas, we'll make crepes, and the toppings will be all different dessert stuff.

PREP TIME
1½ hours
ASSEMBLY TIME
30 minutes

Ingredients

FOR THE PHYLLO "SLAW"

½ cup (1 stick or 113 grams) unsalted butter

Handful of kataifi (shredded phyllo)

2 tablespoons (26 grams) granulated sugar

2 teaspoons (8 grams) ground cinnamon

Pinch of kosher salt

FOR THE FRIED BANANAS

2 slightly ripe bananas

½ cup (1 stick or 113 grams) unsalted butter

¼ cup (100 grams) brown sugar

Pinch of kosher salt

Pinch of orange zest

Pinch of ground cinnamon

FOR THE COCONUT MACAROONS

1⅓ cups (75 grams) sweetened shredded coconut

⅓ cup (67 grams) granulated sugar

2 tablespoons (19 grams) all-purpose flour

Pinch of kosher salt

2 large (80 grams) egg whites

A few drops of pure vanilla extract

FOR THE CREPES

3 tablespoons (42 grams) unsalted butter, melted

2 cups (480 grams) whole milk

4 large eggs

1 tablespoon plus 1 teaspoon (17 grams) granulated sugar

1 teaspoon (5 grams) pure vanilla extract

¼ teaspoon (2 grams) kosher salt

1½ cups (225 grams) all-purpose flour

FOR THE COOKIES

1 recipe Classic Chocolate Chip Cookies (page 29) (you won't need all these cookies, but is there really such a thing as too many cookies?)

OTHER TOPPING IDEAS

Marshmallow cream

Nutella

Buttercream

Whipped cream

Fried pineapple

Fresh fruit

RECIPE CONTINUES →

MAKE THE PHYLLO "SLAW"

1 In a medium sauté pan over medium-high heat, melt the butter.

2 Sprinkle in the kataifi and then add the sugar, cinnamon, and salt.

3 Using a spider or slotted spoon, flip the dough and fry until golden brown on both sides.

4 Drain on paper towels.

MAKE THE FRIED BANANAS

5 Using a chef's knife, slice the bananas into ¼- to ½-inch coins.

6 In a medium sauté pan on medium-high heat, melt the butter and then add the brown sugar and salt.

7 When everything starts bubbling, add the bananas.

8 Using a metal spatula, flip each banana after a minute or so, add the orange zest, and fry for another minute.

9 Remove the bananas, sprinkle with cinnamon, and let them cool on a plate.

Note — *The batter is thin and spreads fast, so be careful.*

MAKE THE MACAROONS

10 Preheat the oven to 325°F. Line a sheet pan with a sheet of parchment paper.

11 In a medium bowl using a wooden spoon or rubber spatula, mix the coconut, sugar, flour, and salt.

12 Add the egg whites and vanilla and mix well.

13 Roll the dough by hand into ping-pong-size balls and place them onto the prepared sheet pan.

14 Bake for 18 to 20 minutes, or until the coconut is nice and brown on top.

MAKE THE CREPES

15 Cut 20 pieces of wax paper into 6-inch squares.

16 Have your cooking spray, two 6-inch nonstick sauté pans, and a rubber spatula at the ready.

17 In a small saucepan over medium heat, melt the butter.

18 In the cup of a blender, blend the milk, eggs, melted butter, sugar, vanilla, salt, and flour until smooth.

19 Transfer the egg mixture to a medium bowl.

20 Spray both sauté pans with cooking spray. Over medium heat, ladle out a few tablespoons of crepe batter into each pan. Swirl the batter around and dump any unused batter back into the bowl.

21 Cook the crepes for 45 seconds, or until firm. Flip, and cook for 30 seconds.

22 On top of a plate, place a piece of wax paper down, put a crepe on it, place another piece of wax paper on top of that, and then repeat.

TO ASSEMBLE THE STREET TACOS

23 Set up a buffet of deliciousness!

24 Crumble up the cookies and put into a small bowl. In 2 other small bowls, add the phyllo "slaw" and macaroons.

25 Serve the bananas on the plate they cooled on.

26 If there's any peanut butter, jelly or maple syrup lying around, add it to your buffet of toppings. Then, holding a crepe in one hand, add fillings to the taco with the other hand. The more items you can stuff into your taco, the happier your belly will be.

27 Go loco!

Duff's Tip

A few of my favorite fixin's include chocolate chip cookies, bananas, and coconut, but you can make up your own! You're the chef; you can put anything you want in your dessert tacos!

CREPES CRAZY!

Crepes are super easy to make and once you have a bunch, you can make all kinds of awesome stuff, like:

1 CHOCOLATE CAKE

Make a whipped ganache or chocolate buttercream, and then spread a tiny bit on a crepe all the way to the edges. Place another crepe on top and do it again. Keep repeating until you have a big solid stack, then ice the whole thing with ganache or buttercream and slice it up.

2 PEACHES-AND-CREAM BURRITOS

Toss some chopped peaches in a little sugar. Whip some cream to soft peaks, and put a little of each into each crepe. Then roll it up like a burrito.

3 BOSTON CREAM CREPES

Fill crepes with vanilla pudding, roll, and drizzle with chocolate ganache.

4 BLUEBERRY-LEMON SOUP DUMPLINGS

Put a spoonful of lemon curd into the middle of a crepe. Drop in some fresh blueberries, gather the edges, and place, upside down, into Asian soup spoons. Slurp.

5 CREPE LASAGNA

Stack crepes using Italian cheese and some tomato sauce. Bake in the oven at 350°F, or until the cheese on top turns golden brown.

6 SUZETTES

Make a compound butter—that's a fancy term for blending yummy things into butter—out of 1 stick (½ cup) unsalted butter, 3 tablespoons of granulated sugar and 1 tablespoon of orange or lemon zest, or anything else you want. Fill each crepe with a little of the butter, fold in half, then fold in half again to make a triangle. Arrange on a sheet pan so they all go the same direction and overlap. Sprinkle with sugar and broil for 2 to 3 minutes, until they're toasty and delicious.

FUDGE

MAKES
48
squares

Mmmmm. Fudge.

PREP TIME
15 minutes

COOKING TIME
10 minutes, plus
2 to 3 hours for
chilling

Ingredients

2 cups (250 grams) chopped walnuts

6 cups (1050 grams) semisweet chocolate chips

Two 14-ounce (794 grams) cans sweetened condensed milk

½ cup (1 stick or 113 grams) unsalted butter

Pinch of kosher salt

1 teaspoon (5 grams) pure vanilla extract

Cooking spray

EQUIPMENT

- 9 × 13-inch baking dish
- Cooking spray
- Sheet pan
- Large pot
- Wax paper
- Wooden spoon

1 Preheat the oven to 350°F. Spray a 9 × 13-inch baking dish with cooking spray and line it with wax paper.

2 Place the walnuts on a sheet pan and toast for 10 minutes, or until they are fragrant and just start turning brown.

3 In a large pot over medium heat, melt the chocolate chips, sweetened condensed milk, butter, and salt. Heat it to just short of a boil, until it's loose and melted.

4 Remove the pot from the heat and, using a wooden spoon, stir in the vanilla and the toasted walnuts.

5 Pour the hot mixture into the prepared baking dish and put in in the fridge until it is cool and set. Cut into 2-inch squares.

I LOVE CANDY

Fun Facts

The inside of a Skittles candy is the same stuff as a Starburst. I like how when you eat too many Skittles, your jaw muscles hurt.

I have no cavities. Brush your teeth.

I LOVE TWIZZLERS because at first, they're really hard and pointy, but once you chew on them, they get soft and mushy.

I LOVE SNICKERS bars because, when you bite into them, the chocolate feels cold on your tongue. Then your teeth snap through the chocolate and then they crunch *and* chew through the caramel and roasted-peanut layers. Then they mush through the nougat (I like the peanut butter nougat).

I LOVE JELLY BEANS, because I love a mystery.

I LOVE GUMMY BEARS because they're squishy and juicy. And it's fun to make them wrestle, and then bite the head off of the loser.

I LOVE REESE'S PEANUT BUTTER CUPS because when you bite them, the inside of your lip hits the tiny, raised, serrated edge of the chocolate, and that feels nice. I also love the saltiness of the peanut butter.

I LOVE GUMMY WORMS because every once in a while, they'll slip between your teeth like delicious dental floss.

You know what's cool about a **KIT KAT BAR**? A piece of a Kit Kat is called a "finger" and the wafers inside are called "bones." And they're filled with broken, mashed-up Kit Kats.

I LOVE SWEDISH FISH because the inside is stretchier than the outside. When you bite one, the inside stretches and the outside kinda breaks apart.

I LOVE FUDGE because it's fudge.

I LOVE SPANGLER CIRCUS PEANUTS because they're kinda gross in a super-sweet and delicious kinda way. They taste like fake bananas.

I LOVE GUMMY SHARKS because they're two colors and each color has a different texture. The white part is kinda creamy and the blue part is sorta fruity and tastes like fake pineapple.

I LOVE RUNTS because I'm always afraid the banana Runts are gonna break a tooth.

I DON'T LOVE NERDS. They're too small.

I LOVE BUTTERFINGER BARS because every bite has a little different texture. Sometimes it's crunchy and sometimes it's soft.

I LOVE CANDY CORN because... just kidding, no one likes candy corn.

I LOVE COW TALES because they're sweet and creamy sticks of caramel and fun to hit my brother, Willie, with.

I LOVE GOLDENBERG'S PEANUT CHEWS because they're really hard to chew and they're not that sweet.

I LOVE JUNIOR MINTS because they always seem like they're a little too big, but when you bite them, they give so easily and they're not too minty.

I LOVE GUMMY ORANGE SLICES because of the way they get stuck in my teeth.

I LOVE SALTWATER TAFFY because when I eat it, I'm usually at the beach.

I LOVE JOLLY RANCHERS because the flavor is super intense, and they get embedded in my molars.

I LOVE WHOPPERS because they're so crunchy and chocolatey and powdery all at the same time.

I LOVE COCA-COLA because there is no meal it doesn't go with, and when it's fresh, it's super bubbly.

DUFF

STUFFED-CRUST DESSERT PIZZA

MAKES

1

10-inch pizza

Pizza is great. But how about pizza for dessert after you eat pizza? One of humankind's greatest achievements is the stuffed-crust pizza. I figured, if they can stuff a crust with cheese and sauce, we can stuff a crust with brownies.

PREP TIME
45 minutes

BAKING TIME
BROWNIE: 40 to 45 minutes
PUFF PASTRY: 20 to 25 minutes

Ingredients

FOR THE TOPPINGS

3 large marshmallows, frozen

Handful of maraschino cherries, stems removed

Cherry jam

FOR THE BROWNIES

¾ cups (170 grams) unsalted butter

9 ounces (255 grams) bittersweet chocolate chips

1½ cups (300 grams) granulated sugar

¾ cup plus 2 tablespoons (180 grams) lightly packed light brown sugar

3 large eggs

2 large (28 grams) yolks

Pinch of kosher salt

1 teaspoon (5 grams) pure vanilla extract

1 cup (150 grams) all-purpose flour

FOR THE REST OF THE STUFFED CRUST

1 recipe Blitz Puff Pastry (page 44), unbaked

1 large egg

Pinch of kosher salt

Pinch of granulated sugar

Splash of water

3 tablespoons sanding sugar

FOR THE RED VELVET SAUCE

½ cup (113 grams) cream cheese, at room temperature

1 teaspoon (5 grams) pure vanilla extract

2½ tablespoons (32 grams) granulated sugar

2½ tablespoons (14 grams) cocoa powder

Pinch of kosher salt

1 cup (236 grams) heavy cream

Few drops of red food coloring

EQUIPMENT

- Resealable freezer bag
- 8- or 9-inch square pan
- Parchment paper
- Small saucepan
- 2 medium bowls
- Whisk
- Rolling pin
- 2 sheet pans
- Small bowl
- Pastry brush
- Potato masher
- Pizza cutter
- Stand mixer
- Rubber spatula
- Kitchen scissors

RECIPE CONTINUES →

1 Put the marshmallows in a resealable freezer bag and pop the bag in the freezer till the marshmallows are frozen, at least 60 minutes.

TO BAKE THE BROWNIES

2 Preheat the oven to 350°F. Grease an 8- or 9-inch square pan and line the bottom with parchment paper.

3 In a small saucepan over medium heat, melt the butter and the chocolate chips together.

4 In a medium bowl, whisk together the sugars, eggs, yolks, salt, and vanilla.

5 Slowly pour the melted butter and chocolate into the egg mixture and whisk till smooth.

6 Add the flour and gently whisk to combine.

7 Pour the batter into the prepared baking pan.

8 Bake for 30 to 40 minutes. (You want these brownies really gooey because you're gonna mash 'em up, so underbake them. I give you permission.) When they're done, let them cool. Then put them in the fridge until they are cool, about 20 minutes.

MAKE THE STUFFED CRUST

9 Heat the oven to 425°F.

10 Using a rolling pin, roll out the puff pastry to ¼-inch thickness.

11 Using a pizza cutter, cut a 10-inch circle. Place the circle of dough on a sheet pan lined with parchment paper. Place the scraps on a sheet pan and put them in the fridge. (Leave the scraps flat; don't bunch them up.)

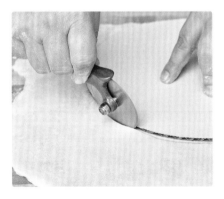

12 In a small bowl using a whisk, make an egg wash by combining the egg, salt, sugar, and water and mixing until smooth.

13 Using a pastry brush, paint the outer edge of the dough with the egg wash.

14 Take the brownies from the fridge and mash them up with a potato masher, so you get a mushy brownie clay. Put aside a handful of mashed brownies for later use (see below), and then use the rest of the brownies to make a tube of brownie clay, about ¾ inch in diameter. Apply the brownie tube ½ inch from the edge of the dough around the entire perimeter.

15 Paint the outside edge with the egg wash again.

16 Take the pan of puff pastry scraps from the fridge. Using a pizza cutter, cut 1½-inch strips and place them over the brownie ring, pressing down on either side of the brownie ring so the strips of dough stick to the egg-washed dough.

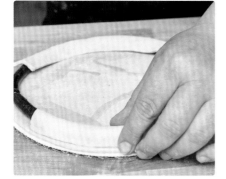

17 You can decorate the crust edge if you want to.

18 Apply egg wash to the top of the stuffed crust and sprinkle the sanding sugar all the way around, so the crust gets crunchy.

19 Bake for 20 to 25 minutes, or until the crust is golden brown.

20 Remove from the oven and set aside to cool.

MAKE THE RED VELVET SAUCE

21 In the bowl of a stand mixer with the paddle attachment, whip on medium-high the cream cheese, vanilla, sugar, cocoa powder, and salt until blended.

22 Scrape the bowl with a rubber spatula and whip on medium-high again until blended.

RECIPE CONTINUES ▶

23 Add the heavy cream and a few drops of red food coloring, and then mix on slow speed to incorporate the color. If you like the color, resume whipping on medium-high speed until stiff peaks form. If you want the color darker, add a few more drops of red food coloring and then increase the speed till you achieve stiff peaks.

24 Spread the red velvet "sauce" on to the crust.

MAKE THE OTHER TOPPINGS

25 For the crumbled "sausage," take the remaining mashed brownies and, using your hands, sprinkle the bits all over the red velvet sauce.

26 For the "cheese," grab the frozen marshmallows from the freezer and cut them up carefully with clean kitchen scissors. Use as many of them as you want. Then, with an adult's help, carefully toast and brown the marshmallows. Work quickly: You don't want to heat up the sauce too much.

27 For the "tomatoes," with the clean kitchen scissors, cut the maraschino cherries into halves and place the halves, cut side down, on the pizza sauce.

28 Now, slice and eat!

Duff's Tip

If you want to add a little green, you can julienne (using a chef's knife, chop into thin strips) some mint. I don't think the flavor goes with the rest of the pizza, but it's your call, Chef.

CHAPTER

5

CUPCAKES

• COOKIES & CREAM •
CUPCAKES

MAKES
16
large-size
cupcakes

I was well into my twenties before I realized that Oreos and cookies-and-cream flavor were basically the same thing—and then I realized that I had the power to make anything Oreo-flavored! So, I'm here now to help you come to this fabulous realization sooner than I did with this fantastic recipe for a cupcake with a cookies-and-cream crust. When I was judging an episode of *Kids Baking Championship*, one of the contestants, Sophie, made a graham cracker crust cupcake that blew my mind. I told her I was going to immediately write a recipe for cookie-crusted cupcakes. This was last night. Thanks, Sophie—inspiration can come from anywhere.

PREP TIME
45 minutes
BAKING TIME
20 to 25 minutes

Ingredients

FOR THE CRUST

20 Oreo cookies (Regular stuffed.)

3 tablespoons (42 grams) unsalted butter, melted

Pinch of kosher salt

FOR THE CUPCAKES

1 cup (150 grams) all-purpose flour

1 cup (200 grams) granulated sugar

⅓ cup plus 1 tablespoon (40 grams) cocoa powder

1 teaspoon (4 grams) baking powder

1 teaspoon (6 grams) baking soda

¼ teaspoon (2 grams) kosher salt

1 large egg

⅓ cup plus 1 tablespoon (80 grams) buttermilk

⅓ cup plus 1 tablespoon (80 grams) warm water

¼ cup (55 grams) vegetable oil

4 tablespoons (56 grams) unsalted butter, melted

1 teaspoon (5 grams) pure vanilla extract

FOR THE CREAM CHEESE FILLING

2 ounces (57 grams) cream cheese, at room temperature

½ cup (110 grams) heavy cream

2 tablespoons (20 grams) powdered sugar

Pinch of kosher salt

Splash of pure vanilla extract

FOR THE AMERICAN BUTTERCREAM

¾ cup (1½ sticks or 170 grams) unsalted butter, at room temperature

2 cups (250 grams) powdered sugar

1 tablespoon (15 grams) whole milk

1 teaspoon (5 grams) pure vanilla extract

Pinch of kosher salt

For decorating (optional):

Leftover Oreo crumbs

6 ounces (170 grams) of coating chocolate

Cookies-and-cream sprinkles

6 ounces (170 grams) shaved chocolate bar

EQUIPMENT

- **16 large-size cupcake liners**
- **Two 8-serving large-size cupcake pans**
- **Food processor**
- **Medium bowl**
- **Wooden spoon**
- **Stand mixer**
- **Rubber spatula**
- **Large muffin scoop**
- **Wire rack**
- **4 plastic piping bags with twist ties**
- **3 large plain piping tips**
- **Melon baller (optional)**

RECIPE CONTINUES

1 Preheat the oven to 325°F. Put 16 paper liners in two 8-serving, large-size-cupcake pans.

MAKE THE OREO CRUST

2 In the bowl of a food processor fitted with a blade attachment, process whole Oreos until they're finely ground (should be crumbly, not mushy). (Do not remove the filling from the cookies.)

3 Remove ½ cup of the Oreo crumbs and set aside.

4 Pour the rest of the crumbs into a medium bowl. Add the melted butter and salt. Using a wooden spoon, mix to combine, and then spoon a few tablespoons into each cupcake liner.

5 Carefully use your fingers to press the crumbs down flat. You can also use the ends of a handleless rolling pin or the bottom of a water glass.

6 Bake for 5 minutes, then remove from the oven and cool.

MAKE THE CUPCAKES

7 In the bowl of a stand mixer with the paddle attachment on low speed, mix together the flour, sugar, cocoa, baking powder, baking soda, and salt. Add the egg, buttermilk, water, oil, butter, and vanilla.

8 Beat on medium speed until smooth.

9 With a rubber spatula, scrape the sides of the bowl, and then beat a little longer, so you know everything is mixed well.

10 Using a large muffin scoop, fill each cup with batter till it's ⅔ full.

11 Bake for 19 to 20 minutes.

Duff's Tip

To test if they're done, stick a toothpick in and see if it comes out clean.

12 Carefully remove the cupcakes from the pan and let them cool on a wire rack.

MAKE THE CREAM CHEESE FILLING

13 In the bowl of a stand mixer with the paddle attachment, whip the cream cheese until it is soft and smooth.

14 Add the heavy cream to the cream cheese and whip until the mix is *almost* done. It should still look a little sloppy and not mmmmmmmmagical.

15 Add the powdered sugar, salt, and vanilla and whip until it's stiff.

16 Transfer the filling to a piping bag (with no tip) and put it in the fridge.

MAKE THE AMERICAN BUTTERCREAM

17 In the bowl of a stand mixer with the paddle attachment, beat the butter on medium-high speed until it's light and fluffy.

18 Add the powdered sugar,

milk, vanilla, and salt and beat on medium speed for 1 minute. Then increase the speed to medium-high and beat for 5 minutes, or until it looks smooth.

19 Transfer the buttercream to 2 or 3 plastic piping bags, each fitted with a large plain piping tip.

20 Secure the ends of the piping bag with twist ties. Do not refrigerate.

TO FINISH THE CUPCAKES

21 Dig a little space in each cupcake. To make the hole, use a big piping tip, melon baller, or even a teaspoon. Repeat with all the cupcakes.

22 Cut the tip off the piping bag and fill the holes with cream cheese filling.

23 Pipe buttercream on top in whatever way you like.

24 You can use the Oreo crumbs that you saved earlier to sprinkle on top *or* you can use cookies-and-cream sprinkles *or* you can use a cheese grater, Microplane, or vegetable peeler to shave a chocolate bar all over the top of the cupcakes. If you want to make a chocolate garnish, melt some coating chocolate and fill a paper piping bag (plastic bags can melt with hot chocolate in them) (instructions on page 21) and pipe thick chocolate squiggles onto a parchment-covered sheet pan. Put the squiggles in the fridge for 15 minutes, then carefully peel them up with an offset spatula and quickly transfer to the tops of the cupcakes.

HOW TO EAT A CUPCAKE
THE DUFF WAY

You've probably seen me eat a cupcake or two on *Kids Baking Championship*. I make a cupcake sandwich and take a big bite. I know it's weird, but this way I keep my nose out of the frosting. It's hard to do with filled cupcakes, but I still like it better than just shoving my face in a cupcake. Here's how to do it:

STEP

1

Remove any excess frosting with your finger. Lick your finger. Now you have control over the ratio of frosting to cupcake.

STEP

2

Make a claw with each hand so you can get your fingers spaced evenly around the equator of the cupcake. Gently apply even pressure and tear the cupcake in half into top and bottom halves.

STEP

3

Create the sandwich by flipping the bottom of the cupcake, torn side down, onto the frosting on top half of the cupcake.

STEP

4

Open your mouth and your eyes as wide as you can and take a bite.

UNICORN CUPCAKES

MAKES

12

cupcakes

Unicorns actually poop rainbow cupcakes, but they're also hard to find. If you really need a rainbow cupcake, this recipe will have to do. These are fun though, 'cause you actually make cute little unicorn ears and horns to go with them. So if you're ever walking in the woods and you see a rainbow cupcake lying on the ground, it's probably delicious, but it also might have come out of the back end of a unicorn.

PREP TIME
2 hours
BAKING TIME
15 to 18 minutes

Ingredients

FOR THE DECORATIONS

16-ounce package mini marshmallows

2 tablespoons (30 grams) water, plus more as needed

8 cups (960 grams) powdered sugar

Pinch of kosher salt

½ cup (95 grams) vegetable shortening

Pink food coloring

Edible gold paint (optional)

Edible glitter (optional)

FOR THE CUPCAKES

1½ cups (225 grams) all-purpose flour

1½ teaspoons (6 grams) baking powder

Pinch of kosher salt

2 large eggs, at room temperature

⅔ cup (133 grams) granulated sugar

¾ cup (1½ sticks or 170 grams) butter, melted

2 teaspoons (9 grams) pure vanilla extract

Pink food coloring

Orange food coloring

Yellow food coloring

FOR THE BUTTERCREAM

1½ cups (3 sticks or 339 grams) butter, at room temperature

¼ teaspoon (2 grams) kosher salt

1 tablespoon (14 grams) pure vanilla extract

1 to 2 tablespoons (14 to 28 grams) whole milk

4 cups (480 grams) powdered sugar

Pink food coloring

Orange food coloring

Yellow food coloring

EQUIPMENT

- Large microwave-safe bowl
- Rubber spatula
- Sandwich bags
- 4 medium bowls
- 4 small bowls
- Stand mixer
- 12 paper cupcake liners
- 12-serving cupcake pan
- Whisk
- Wire rack
- 5 piping bags
- Grass piping tip
- Twelve 12-inch bamboo skewers
- Small piece of Styrofoam
- Small knife or scissors
- Parchment paper
- Small offset spatula
- Cookie cutter
- Rolling pin

RECIPE CONTINUES

MAKE THE MARSHMALLOW FONDANT

1 Place the marshmallows and water in a large microwave-safe bowl.

2 Microwave on high for 30 seconds and then, with a rubber spatula, stir really well. Microwave for another 30 seconds and then stir again. Repeat until the marshmallows are melted and smooth.

3 Pour in 5 cups of the powdered sugar and, using a wooden spoon, slowly stir to combine.

4 Rub some shortening on the counter (make sure the surface is clean) and all over your hands.

5 Turn out the marshmallow mixture onto the table and knead with your hands.

6 Rub some shortening on the white marshmallow fondant, place the fondant in separate resealable plastic bags, and set the bags aside.

Duff's Tip

If the marshmallow mixture feels too dry, add a few drops of water. If it feels too wet, add more powdered sugar.

MAKE THE CUPCAKES

7 Preheat the oven to 350°F. Insert paper liners into a standard 12-serving cupcake pan and set the pan aside.

8 In a medium bowl, whisk together the flour, baking powder, and salt.

9 In the bowl of a stand mixer with the paddle attachment on medium-high speed, beat the eggs, granulated sugar, butter, and vanilla until it's light and creamy.

10 A few spoonfuls at a time, add the flour mixture into the egg mixture while beating on medium-low, until it is all combined.

11 Divide the batter into 3 medium bowls. Whisk into the first bowl a few drops of orange food coloring. Repeat with the yellow and pink colors in the other bowls.

12 Drop a few spoonfuls of each color batter into each cup of the prepared cupcake pan, filling about ⅔ of the way.

13 Bake for 15 to 18 minutes or until a toothpick inserted into the middle of a cupcake comes out clean.

14 Remove from the oven and turn the cupcakes out onto a wire rack to cool.

MAKE THE RAINBOW BUTTERCREAM

15 In the bowl of the stand mixer using the paddle attachment on low speed, beat the butter, salt, vanilla, and milk until it is light and fluffy.

16 Add the powdered sugar, a little at a time, while still mixing on low speed.

17 After all the powdered sugar is added, mix on medium-high speed for a few seconds till the buttercream is well combined.

18 Divide the buttercream into 4 small bowls. Mix a few drops of pink color into 1 of the bowls and blend well. Repeat with the orange and yellow buttercream. (The fourth bowl has the white buttercream.)

19 Fill each of 3 piping bags with a colored buttercream. Snip the pointy end of each piping bag with scissors. Then fit 1 piping bag with a grass tip.

20 Insert the 3 piping bags into the bag with grass tip and carefully squeeze out the buttercream into the grass-tipped bag so all three colors run in a stripe next to each other. Cinch off the back of the bag with a twist tie and set aside. Discard the empty bags.

MAKE THE UNI-HORNS

21 Get your hands on some bamboo skewers and a piece of Styrofoam.

22 Place 12 skewers in a bowl of water, with the sharp ends sticking out of the water and the blunt ends in the water. Let the skewers soak while you do the next step, or for at least 15 minutes.

23 Using the marshmallow fondant, roll out twelve 8-inch snakes that are ¼ inch thick at one end and taper to ⅛ inch at the other.

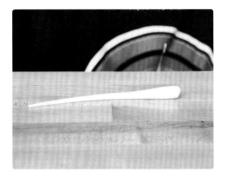

24 Attach the skinny end of a snake to the wet, blunt end of a skewer, then twirl the whole snake in tight coils around the wet part of the skewer. (A portion of the skewer should be sticking out at the bottom.) Repeat with the other 11 snakes.

25 If you are using edible gold paint, paint each uni-horn gold.

26 Gently stick the pointy end of all the skewers into the Styrofoam and let the uni-horns dry for at least 60 minutes.

TO MAKE UNICORN EARS

27 Using a rolling pin, roll out a piece of white fondant to ⅛-inch thickness.

28 Using a cookie cutter, cut out a small football-shaped piece of fondant (about ¾ × ¾ inches). Then cut the point off one end of the football. Now you have a unicorn ear.

29 Set the unicorn ears aside on a piece of parchment paper to dry.

TO ASSEMBLE UNICORN CUPCAKES

30 Using a filled piping bag and small offset spatula, ice each cooled cupcake with the white buttercream.

31 Cut the ends of the skewers so you have about 2 inches of skewer showing under each uni-horn.

32 Stick the uni-horn into the center of the cupcake just in front of where the mane starts.

33 Starting in the center of each cupcake, pipe a rainbow mane on each cupcake. Make sure to flare it out to one side.

34 Place an ear on either side of the uni-horn.

35 If you are using edible glitter, sprinkle a little onto each cupcake.

36 Let the magic begin!

UNICORN FACTS

DID YOU KNOW?

Unicorn horns are called *alicorns*.

Unicorns live on every continent except maybe Antarctica. I've never seen one there.

Unicorns live for hundreds of years.

Unicorn eyes are usually sky blue or lavender.

Unicorns absorb their cosmic energy from the universe through their horn.

Unicorns can be any color! White, silver, gold, brown, black, or anything else.

If you tell a lie to a unicorn, it will pierce your heart with its horn.

Baby unicorns are called sparkles.

The ancient Greeks knew that unicorns were real.

Unicorns have aquatic mammal cousins called narwhals.

If a unicorn has wings, it's also called an alicorn. These are usually the offspring of a Pegasus and a unicorn.

If you are wounded and a unicorn touches your wound with its horn, you heal.

If you drink out of a unicorn-horn cup, you cannot be poisoned.

Unicorn in Chinese is *qilin* or *ch'i-lin*.

Unicorns are the national animal of Scotland. April 9 is National Unicorn Day in Scotland.

The first known painting of a unicorn is from 15,000 years ago and was found in a cave in France.

In the 5th century BCE, a Greek historian saw a white rhino in Persia and thought it was a unicorn.

Vikings used to sell narwhal horns as unicorn horns.

Throughout history, unicorns have been depicted as horses, goats, sheep, cows, and even buffaloes.

Mermaid unicorns are commonly referred to as *mermacorns*.

CHRISTMAS TREE

MAKES
1
2-foot tree with 24 mini cupcakes

Sometimes you just don't know what to do with a bunch of cupcakes. You stick 'em on a platter; people eat them; you wash the platter. I like the cupcake Christmas tree for serving because it's fun to build, but it's even more fun to take apart.

PREP TIME
15 minutes, plus 45 minutes for constructing the tree

BAKING TIME
12 to 15 minutes

Ingredients

FOR THE MINI CUPCAKES

2 ounces (57 grams) bittersweet chocolate chips

¼ cup (59 grams) hot brewed coffee

¼ cup (46 grams) lightly packed light brown sugar

¼ cup (23 grams) cocoa powder

1 large egg

1 large egg yolk

¼ cup (54 grams) vegetable oil

¼ cup (60 grams) buttermilk

1 teaspoon (5 grams) pure vanilla extract

½ cup (75 grams) all-purpose flour

¼ cup (50 grams) granulated sugar

Pinch of kosher salt

¼ teaspoon (2 grams) baking soda

FOR THE AMERICAN BUTTERCREAM

1½ cups (3 sticks or 339 grams) unsalted butter, at room temperature

1 tablespoon (14 grams) pure vanilla extract

¼ teaspoon (2 grams) kosher salt

4 cups (500 grams) powdered sugar

1 tablespoon (14 grams) whole milk, plus more as needed

Food coloring (optional)

FOR THE DECORATIONS

Nonpareils or sprinkles

Peppermint candies

Sixlets

Anything else you want

EQUIPMENT

- 24 mini-cupcake liners (pick something cool, like shiny ones!)
- Mini-cupcake pan
- Large bowl
- Whisk
- Small muffin scoop
- Wire rack
- Stand mixer
- Rubber spatula
- Small bowls
- Piping bags
- Various piping tips

EXTRAS

2-foot Styrofoam cone wrapped in plastic (with at least a 4-inch-wide base)

Wrapping paper of your choice

Transparent wrapping tape

24 or more 4-inch double-sided toothpicks

RECIPE CONTINUES

MAKE THE CUPCAKES

1 Preheat the oven to 325°F.

2 Line a 24-cup mini-cupcake pan with liners.

3 In a large bowl, carefully combine the chocolate chips and hot coffee.

4 Let the chocolate melt, then stir in the brown sugar and cocoa powder.

5 Then whisk in the egg, egg yolk, oil, buttermilk, and vanilla.

6 Next whisk in the flour, granulated sugar, salt, and baking powder.

7 Using a small muffin scoop, scoop the batter into all the mini-cupcake liners till ⅔ full.

To me, it's easier if you fill a pastry bag with batter and pipe the cups slowly.

8 Bake the cupcakes for 12 to 15 minutes or until a toothpick inserted into the cupcake comes out clean.

9 Carefully remove the pan from the oven and let the cupcakes cool in the pan for 10 minutes, turn them out of the pan, and then move them to a wire rack to cool completely.

MAKE THE AMERICAN BUTTERCREAM

10 In the bowl of a stand mixer using the paddle attachment at medium speed, beat the butter, vanilla, and salt until it is light and fluffy.

11 On low speed, slowly add the powdered sugar. After all the powdered sugar has been added, add 1 tablespoon of milk at a time till the buttercream reaches a pipeable consistency.

12 Mix on medium-high for a few seconds. At this point, if you want to make different colors of buttercream, separate the buttercream into small bowls and add the food coloring you want.

ICE AND DECORATE YOUR CUPCAKES

13 Using a rubber spatula, put your buttercream in a few different pastry bags, depending on how many different colors you have, fitted with different tips.

14 Pipe frosting onto each cupcake in a fun pattern.

15 Decorate each cupcake with the candies and sprinkles you chose.

Note

Remember, one of these cupcakes will be the one on top of your cupcake Christmas tree—so plan ahead!

RECIPE CONTINUES

MAKE THE CHRISTMAS TREE

16 Use a glue gun (following the safety tips on page 121) to affix the wrapping paper of your choice to the Styrofoam cone (don't remove the cone's plastic wrapping). Trim the extra and make sure it is wrinkle free and clean.

17 Stick 24 toothpicks about 1 inch into the foam in a random order but with enough space between them for all the cupcakes to fit. (Make sure to put one on top!)

19 And don't forget to finish by adding your "star"—a final cupcake on the top!

18 Pipe on a buttercream garland to decorate the tree. And finally, stick on all the cupcakes! A delicious Christmas tree!

HOT GLUE
DO's & DON'Ts

DO

Make sure you always have an adult around before you use hot glue.

DO

Allow your gun to warm up before you try to use it.

DO

Put a glue stick into the gun before you turn it on.

DO

Use the stand for the gun.

DON'T

Let glue touch anything you want people to eat.

DON'T

Plug in the gun and then get your paper ready. Do your mise en place first.

DON'T

Lay it on its side. Use the stand.

DON'T

Touch the tip of the glue gun. It's hot and hot glue is super sticky, like lava.

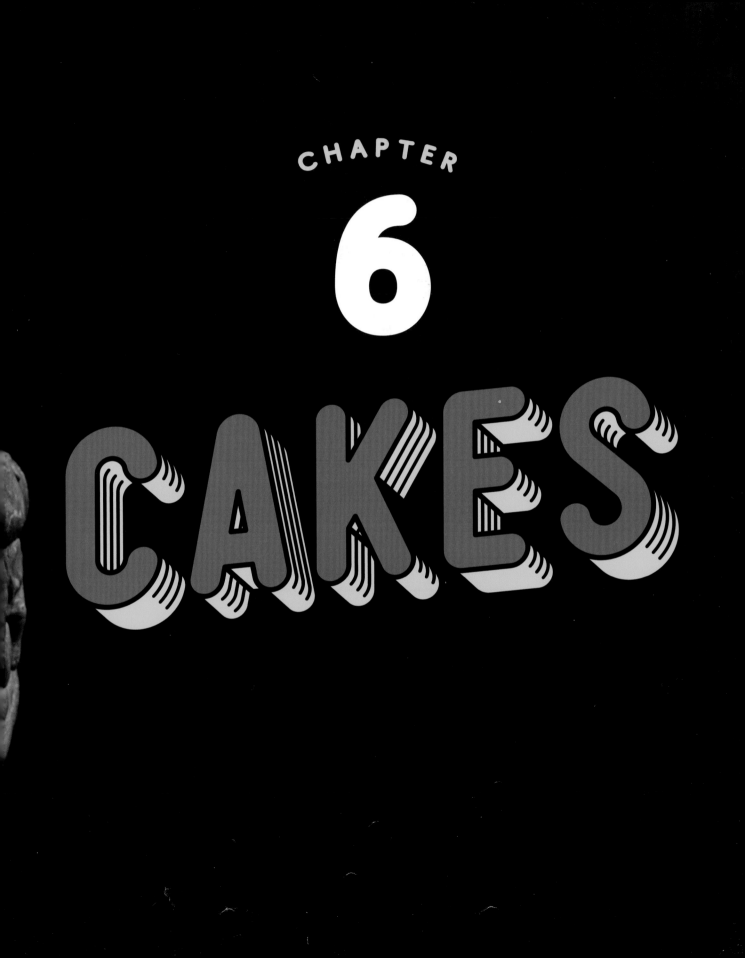

CHAPTER

6

CAKES

CAKE BASICS

Baking cakes is its own weird subset of baking.
There are lots of terms and pieces of equipment to know.
Here's a list of the things any baker needs to be
familiar with in order to be good at baking cakes:

CAKE PANS: These can be round or square or any shape you can imagine. You want to get good, heavy ones, so your cakes bake evenly. Cheap, thin cake pans don't last long, and they can bake your cakes unevenly. Some recipes call for buttering and flouring the pan. This means rubbing a small amount of butter all over the inside of the cake pan to get it nice and greasy, then putting a little flour in the pan and covering every inch of the butter. Then you shake out any excess flour.

CAKE SAW: A cake saw has one or more blades suspended between two handles. Using a cake saw creates a level slice. It's nice to have, but I prefer to use a long, serrated knife (like a bread knife).

CAKE TURNTABLE: Cake turntables spin freely, allowing you to rotate your cake to ice and decorate it more easily.

CAKE TESTER: This is anything you stick into a cake to see if it's done. There are specially made cake testers out there, but bamboo skewers or long toothpicks work just fine.

COOLING RACK: After a cake comes out of the oven and cools for a few minutes, it's best to turn the cakes out onto a wire cooling rack. In addition to allowing the cake to cool outside the pan, this tool keeps the cake from steaming on the bottom and getting soggy.

SWISS, FRENCH, AND ITALIAN BUTTERCREAM: These are types of cake frostings. They are lighter than all-butter American buttercream. Try making some and see what kind you prefer.

CAKE RING: This is basically a cake pan with no bottom. You don't put a cake ring in the oven. It is used for cutting cake rounds out of larger cakes and for building mousse cakes and layered desserts called entremets.

ICING AND FROSTING: This is weird, but you generally ice a cake using frosting. Icing, the verb, is what you do to a cake. Icing, the noun, is synonymous with glaze and is thinner and shinier than frosting and is generally used for pastries. Donut glaze, for example, is an icing. Buttercream is a frosting. But the act of spreading frosting on a cake is called icing.

CAKE ROUNDS: Cake rounds are pieces of cardboard that are cut into circles to support individual cake layers as they are being filled and decorated. The rounds are generally not used in a finished, assembled cake.

CRUMB COAT: This is a thin layer of buttercream applied before you ice a cake. Bakers do this to keep all the crumbs stuck to the cake and out of the frosting.

ROLLED FONDANT (PRONOUNCED "FAWN-DENT," NOT "FAHN-DAHNT"): Fondant is a smooth, rolled icing that covers cakes to make them easy to decorate, and to keep them fresh longer.

GUM PASTE: Weird word, right? It's a sweet, claylike dough that dries into whatever shape you make it. It's great for making flowers and stuff as cake decorations.

ROYAL ICING: Royal Icing is wetter than buttercream. It's used for fine piping and decorating cakes and cookies. Royal icing is made with egg whites and powdered sugar or meringue powder and dries to a hard, brittle decoration.

CAKE STAND: A decorative plate, usually on a pedestal, that is used to show off a decorated cake.

AIRBRUSH: This is a fun method of applying color to cakes and cake decorations. Using a small nozzle attached to an air compressor, it sprays liquid color directly onto whatever you are trying to paint.

TYPES OF CAKES

Cake is broad term and can mean lots of different things. Get to know, to bake and taste, all the different kinds of cakes and find out which you like the most.

HIGH-RATIO CAKE: These are the cakes you are probably the most familiar with. Cake mixes and most regular bakery cakes are high-ratio cakes. The sugar in these cakes equals or exceeds the flour by weight. High-ratio cakes are very sweet, and the crumb is denser.

POUND CAKE: These are cakes that have equal portions of flour, butter, sugar, and eggs. These cakes are also dense and sweet. Pound cakes are commonly glazed and are good for serving with coffee or tea.

BUTTER CAKE: Butter cakes are generally the kinds of cakes most people make at home. These use butter or another solid fat as the fat in the recipe.

SPONGE CAKE: This is any cake that rises, because the eggs are whipped and folded in rather than using baking soda and baking powder to cause leavening. A French genoise is a sponge cake. Sponge cakes tend to be drier than high-ratio cakes and usually require some simple-syrup to keep them moist.

ANGEL FOOD CAKE: This is a type of sponge cake that only has egg whites, no yolks. It's very light and airy and is delicious with whipped cream and strawberries.

BISCUIT CAKE: This is yet another type of sponge cake, but it has had the whites and yolks whipped separately.

CHIFFON: A hybrid cake containing oil, baking powder, and whipped egg whites and yolks. The texture is very light, but the flavor is nice and rich.

FLOURLESS CAKE: These cakes are made with eggs but no flour. They are denser than sponge cakes. Cheesecakes are a type of flourless cake.

THE SCIENCE OF CAKES

Most of the cakes we're gonna bake rise because of baking soda or baking powder. Some cakes rise because of the air that is whipped into them. And some cakes rise because of yeast. All these are just different methods of getting air into the batter. Here's the science of why cakes rise:

CHEMICAL LEAVENING: There are basically two types of chemical leavening agents that you're ever going to use: baking powder and baking soda. Baking soda is a base, which means when you mix it with anything acidic, such as vinegar or lemon juice, it makes carbon dioxide bubbles. These bubbles grow inside your cake batter and make it rise as it bakes. Cakes with baking soda always have some acidic ingredient like brown sugar, buttermilk, yogurt, vinegar, or honey, which creates a reaction in the batter. Baking powder, on the other hand, is a mixture of baking soda and cream of tartar. Cream of tartar is an acid, the soda is the base, and the two react when the baking powder gets wet. Baking powder usually says "double acting" on the can, because it makes cakes rise when the batter gets wet *and* when it gets hot.

MECHANICAL LEAVENING: Mechanical leavening happens with no help from ingredients. It is purely the forces of physics at work. When air gets hot, it expands. If hot air is trapped inside of cake batter, the batter rises. Same thing with steam. As water converts to steam as it heats, it expands as well. This is how pâte à choux rises. There are lots of ways to get air into a batter. Creaming butter and sugar, whipping eggs, kneading, and mixing all add air into the batter so that it rises.

BIOLOGICAL LEAVENING: This is when you have a batter with yeast in it. The yeast is a single-celled fungus that eats sugar and converts it into carbon dioxide. The more sugar the yeast eats, the more gas it releases, and the higher things rise.

HOW TO FILL, STACK, ICE, AND DECORATE A CAKE

The first step in decorating a cake is getting it built and ready for decoration. It's super simple, but it does require some practice. Just keep trying, and eventually your cakes will look perfect.

STACKING AND FILLING: We talk about how to do this on page 22. So look there!

CRUMB-COATING: We talk about how to do this on page 20. So look there!

ICING: We talk about how to do this on page 20. So look there!

PIPING A BORDER: We talk about how to do this on page 21. So look there!

APPLYING ROLLED FONDANT: Wash your hands—anything stuck to your hands will end up in the fondant. Then take a chunk of fondant and knead it a few times to get it pliable and smooth, but don't knead it too much, or else it will overheat and start coming

apart. Sprinkle some cornstarch onto a flat surface and push the chunk of fondant down so you have a rough circle. Using a rolling pin and starting in the center, roll the fondant out and away from you. Rotate the fondant 180 degrees and repeat. Next, rotate 90 degrees, roll it, and then rotate 180 degrees and roll another time. Repeat this process until you have a rough circle approximately ¼ inch thick. Measure the sides and top of your cake and make sure that the fondant will cover the whole thing. Drape the fondant over your chilled cake, getting it as centered as possible. Quickly smooth any bubbles out from the top of the cake, then, using your hands, smooth the fondant on the top corner edge of the cake. Next, smooth out the next few inches down the side of the cake, turning the cake constantly. Keep going all the way around the cake and all the way down until you hit the bottom. Using a sharp knife, trim the excess fondant about ¼ inch above the bottom of the cake. This will allow for the cake to settle without buckling the fondant. Finally, use a fondant smoother to really get the sides and top flat and even.

· CHOCOLATE ·
BUNDT CAKE

MAKES
1
10-cup
Bundt cake

There's something about Bundt cakes that are just more delicious. Maybe it's that they bake faster than regular cakes. Maybe it's 'cause there's a hole in the middle of them and so they stay super moist inside and crusty outside. Or maybe it's that there's no end piece. The world will never know for sure, but regardless, Bundt cakes are super good.

PREP TIME
2 hours
BAKING TIME
50 to 55 minutes

Ingredients

FOR THE CAKE

1 cup (227 grams) brewed coffee

1 cup (2 sticks or 227 grams) unsalted butter

¾ cup (64 grams) Dutch-process cocoa

2 cups (400 grams) granulated sugar

¾ teaspoon (3 grams) baking powder

¼ teaspoon (2 grams) baking soda

¼ teaspoon (2 grams) kosher salt

1½ cups (245 grams) all-purpose flour

2 large eggs

½ cup (113 grams) sour cream

2 teaspoons (9 grams) pure vanilla extract

FOR THE GANACHE

4 ounces (113 grams) semisweet chocolate chips

2 ounces (57 grams) heavy cream

Powdered sugar, for dusting (optional)

EQUIPMENT

- 10-cup Bundt pan
- Large bowl
- 2 medium bowls
- Small bowl
- Whisk
- Medium saucepan
- Wire rack

RECIPE CONTINUES →

MAKE THE BUNDT CAKE

1 Preheat the oven to 350°F. Spray a Bundt pan with cooking spray and set aside.

2 In a small saucepan over low heat, melt the butter, then add the coffee and cocoa and whisk until smooth.

3 In a medium bowl, whisk together the sugar, baking powder, baking soda, salt, and flour.

4 Pour the coffee mixture into the flour mixture and then whisk until smooth.

5 In another medium bowl, whisk together the eggs, sour cream, and vanilla.

6 Pour the egg mixture into the coffee-flour mixture and whisk until smooth.

7 Pour the batter into the Bundt pan and bake for 50 to 55 minutes, or until a skewer inserted into the cake comes out clean.

8 Carefully remove the Bundt cake and cool it in the pan for 5 minutes before turning it over onto a wire rack. Wait 10 minutes before lifting the Bundt pan off the cake.

MAKE THE GANACHE

9 Put the chocolate chips in a medium bowl and set aside.

10 Pour the cream into a saucepan and, over medium-high heat, bring the cream to a boil.

11 Turn off the heat and pour the cream over the chocolate chips. Cover the bowl with a kitchen towel and let it sit for 3 minutes.

12 Whisk the ganache until it's shiny.

ICE THE CAKE

13 While the ganache is still warm but the cake is cool, spoon the icing over the cake, letting it drip down the sides.

14 After the ganache has set, dust a little powdered sugar over the top of the cake.

Duff's Tip

Let the cake cool completely, at least 1 hour, before icing.

CONFETTI CAKE

MAKES

1

2-layer, 9-inch round cake

Most of the time, when you get a cake, you're celebrating something. Sometimes when you celebrate things, people throw confetti. I like putting the confetti right in the cake because, that way, no one has to throw confetti and I don't have to sweep it up after the party.

PREP TIME
1 hour
BAKING TIME
25 to 30 minutes

Ingredients

FOR THE CAKE

1 cup (240 grams) whole milk, at room temperature

6 large (170 to 180 grams) egg whites, at room temperature

2 teaspoons (5 grams) pure vanilla extract

2¼ cups (290 grams) cake flour

1¾ cups (350 grams) granulated sugar

1 tablespoon plus 1 teaspoon (16 grams) baking powder

1 teaspoon (6 grams) salt

¾ cup (1½ sticks or 170 grams) unsalted butter, at room temperature

½ cup (80 grams) rainbow sprinkles

FOR THE AMERICAN BUTTERCREAM

1½ cups (339 grams) unsalted butter, at room temperature

4 cups (500 grams) powdered sugar

¼ teaspoon (2 grams) kosher salt

1 tablespoon (14 grams) pure vanilla extract

1 tablespoon (14 grams) whole milk

Rainbow sprinkles

EQUIPMENT

- Two 9-inch round cake pans
- Cooking spray
- Two 9-inch parchment rounds
- Medium bowl
- Whisk
- Stand mixer
- Rubber spatula
- Metal spatula
- Serrated knife or cake saw
- Cardboard cake round
- Cake turntable or flat plate
- Piping bag
- Large plain or star piping tip

RECIPE CONTINUES

MAKE THE CAKE

1 Preheat the oven to 350°F. Prepare two 9-inch round cake pans by greasing the pans with cooking spray and putting a circle of parchment paper onto the bottom of each pan.

2 In a medium bowl, whisk together the milk, egg whites, and vanilla.

3 In the bowl of a stand mixer using the paddle attachment on medium speed, combine the flour, sugar, baking powder, and salt.

4 Add the butter, and then beat on low until the mixture looks like wet sand.

5 Slowly add the milk mixture and combine on medium-low speed until the batter looks smooth and creamy, for about 3 minutes. Take the bowl from the stand mixer.

6 Add sprinkles and then, using a rubber spatula, fold the sprinkles a few times. Divide the cake batter between the 2 pans.

7 Bake for roughly 25 minutes, or until a skewer inserted into the cake comes out clean.

8 Cool on a wire rack.

MAKE THE FROSTING

9 In the bowl of a stand mixer with the paddle attachment at medium speed, beat the butter until it is smooth, creamy, and light yellow in color.

10 Add the powdered sugar a few tablespoons at a time. Using a rubber spatula, scrape the side of the bowl and the paddle after the 4 cups of powdered sugar have been added.

11 Add the salt and vanilla. Scrape the bowl and the paddle.

12 Add the milk. Scrape the bowl and paddle again.

13 If the buttercream seems too loose, add more powdered sugar; if it's too dry, add a few more drops of milk.

TO ASSEMBLE THE CAKE

14 Using a long, serrated knife or cake saw, cut the dome off of the top of the cakes.

15 Put one cake layer, cut side up, on a cardboard cake round, then place on top of a cake turntable or flat plate.

16 Put a small amount of buttercream in a separate bowl. Using a metal spatula, spread the buttercream about ¾ inch thick over the top of the layer. (This is the crumb coat and will keep crumbs from infecting the rest of your buttercream.) Top with some confetti or rainbow sprinkles.

17 Place the next cake, cut side down, on top of the bottom layer. Bend down, get at eye level with the cake, and look for any bumps or unevenness on the top. Level it by gently pushing any spot that looks wonky.

18 Using the metal spatula, apply buttercream from the separate bowl to ice a very thin layer on the top and side of the cake.

19 Refrigerate for 15 to 20 minutes.

20 Using a metal spatula for a smoother look or a rubber spatula for a more rustic look, ice the outside of your cake.

21 Fit a piping bag with a large plain or star tip and put the remaining buttercream in the bag. Pipe a border around the cake.

22 Decorate with sprinkles, stick some candles in it, sing some songs, play some silly games, and have a party.

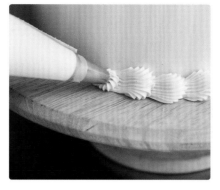 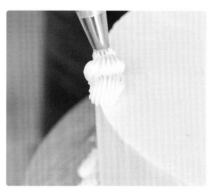

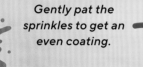

Gently pat the sprinkles to get an even coating.

Scrape the sides of the bowl and the beater every time you add something.

CLEMENTINE CAKE

I was watching this Ben Stiller movie called *The Secret Life of Walter Mitty*, and in the movie, there was a clementine cake. They talked about it a few different times, and it seemed that the clementine cake was important to the story. I had never heard of clementine cake, but seeing how I am the cake guy, I felt it was my duty to know what this thing was. So I found a recipe, and I made it. It was delicious. After you boil the clementines, your house smells like fruity butter. This is now one of my favorite cakes to bake—and it's also one of my favorite movies!

PREP TIME
15 minutes
COOKING TIME
2 hours
BAKING TIME
1 hour

Ingredients

FOR THE CAKE

1 pound (454 grams) seedless clementines

1 cup plus 2 tablespoons (225 grams) granulated sugar

2⅓ cups (250 grams) almond flour

6 large eggs

Pinch of kosher salt

1½ teaspoons (6 grams) baking powder

Few drops pure vanilla extract

FOR THE BUTTERCREAM

¾ cup (1½ sticks or 170 grams) unsalted butter, at room temperature

Pinch of kosher salt

1½ teaspoons (7 grams) pure vanilla extract

2 cups (250 grams) powdered sugar

1 tablespoon (14 grams) whole milk

FOR THE DECORATIONS

1 lemon

1 lime

1 navel orange

1 blood orange

4 cups (944 grams) water

4 cups (800 grams) granulated sugar

Lime leaves, for garnish (optional)

EQUIPMENT

- Large pot
- Wire mesh strainer or colander
- Two 9-inch round cake pans
- Cooking spray
- Two 9-inch round pieces parchment
- Wire cooling rack
- Food processor
- Stand mixer
- Chef's knife
- Cutting board
- Wide pot
- Tongs
- Sheet pan
- Parchment paper
- 2 cardboard cake rounds
- Cake turntable or flat plate
- Metal spatula

RECIPE CONTINUES

Note

*There's no flour in
the recipe!*

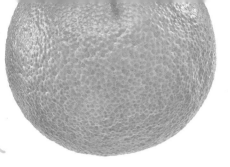

MAKE THE CLEMENTINE CAKE

1 Fill a large pot with 4 quarts of water and bring the water to a boil.

2 Add the clementines to the water, reduce the heat to medium, and cook for 2 hours. (Warning: It will smell amazing!)

3 Drain the clementines in a wire mesh strainer or colander and allow to cool. If there's seeds, cut the clementines open and remove them.

4 Preheat the oven to 350°F. Grease two 9-inch round cake pans with cooking spray and cover the bottom of each pan with a parchment circle.

5 In the bowl of a food processor with a blade attachment, add the clementines and pulse until you get a paste.

6 Add the granulated sugar, almond flour, eggs, salt, baking powder, and vanilla and pulse until the batter is well combined.

7 Pour the batter evenly into the cake pans and bake for 35 to 40 minutes.

8 Allow the cakes to cool on a wire cooling rack.

MAKE THE BUTTERCREAM

9 In the bowl of a stand mixer using the paddle attachment on medium speed, beat the butter, salt, and vanilla until the mixture is light and fluffy.

10 Turn the speed to low and add the powdered sugar a few tablespoons at a time.

11 When all the powdered sugar is added, mix on medium-high for a few seconds. If it isn't smooth and creamy, add 1 tablespoon of milk.

Duff's Tip

The tops of the cakes will get dark. I think it's delicious when the cake top is dark, but, if you don't like it dark, cover the tops with foil for the last 15 to 20 minutes of baking.

TO CANDY THE CITRUS

12 Using a chef's knife and a cutting board, slice the citrus into thin slices. If there's seeds, remove them.

13 In a wide pot over medium-high heat, add the water and sugar and heat until the sugar is dissolved and the mixture is simmering.

14 Using tongs, carefully set the citrus slices into the water without overlapping.

15 Turn down the heat to low and let the slices soak up the sugar water, turning them once.

16 Once the rinds become translucent, after about 90 minutes, take out the slices and let them cool on a sheet pan lined with parchment paper.

ASSEMBLE THE CAKE

17 Place the bottom layer of cake on a cake round, and then place on a cake turntable or flat plate.

18 Using a metal spatula, spread half of the frosting on one of the cakes and put the second cake layer on top. Then spread the remaining frosting on top of that.

19 Arrange the candied citrus (we just used clementines but you can use whatever citrus you like) on top of the cake in a fun pattern. If the whole slices won't fit, you can cut them with a chef's knife.

20 If you have some lime leaves, put some around the cake for garnish.

BISON CAKE

I have a little bison who goes everywhere with me. His name is Carl. He lives in my backpack. I bet you have a favorite animal. This is how I make a cake that looks like Carl. You can make a bison, they're really the best animal ever, or, you can make your favorite animal by using the bison as a guide.

THE CAKES: Bake three 6-inch round cakes, any flavor you like. Stack, fill, and ice the layers according to the directions on pages 20 and 22. Refrigerate the cake on a piece of parchment for at least 45 minutes while you color your fondant and make some decorations.

THE FONDANT: Using a ball of fondant about the size of a big apple, color it light brown by kneading a little brown food coloring into it **1** **2**. Dye another ball the same size a much darker brown by using brown food coloring, plus a little bit of red food coloring and a little bit of black food coloring. If the dark brown is too red, add a little green food coloring

to counteract the red. Place the fondant balls in separate resealable plastic bags and set aside. Now using a ball of fondant about the size of a walnut, color it black. Color a golf ball–size ball with green food coloring. Place these balls in separate resealable plastic bags.

START DECORATING: Using a rolling pin, roll out the light brown fondant by following the directions on page 126. Roll out to a 16-inch circle **3** and drape over the cake, trimming any excess about ¼ inch from the bottom **4**. (Save any scraps for later to make bison ears.) Roll out the green fondant into a circle at least 11 inches across. Dab a little water onto the surface of a 10-inch circle of ¼-inch-thick

foam core. Brush off any excess cornstarch from the green fondant and lay it on the foam core. Smooth it out and trim it so it is the same size as the foam core. Now the buffalo has some grass to lay down in. Brush a little bit of water onto the grass. Discard the parchment from the cake and place the brown cake in the middle of the grass.

THE HORNS & EARS: Make two little buffalo horns by shaping some white fondant into a horn shape with your fingers and sticking a toothpick into the fat end of the horn **5** **6**. Set these aside to dry for 30 minutes. Next, roll out a small piece of the light brown fondant and cut out two circles **7**.

Trim one-quarter of the circle away and gently fold the remaining three-quarters circle to form a little buffalo ear **8**. Repeat with the other circle. Set These aside to dry for 30 minutes.

With a tiny drop of water, fasten the horns and ears where you think they should go. I like putting the ears at a 45-degree angle on the top corner of the cake, with the horns in between **9**.

THE EYES & FACE: Make the bison's face. To make his eyes, roll out a piece of white fondant and cut two circles about the size of a quarter **10**. Now, make two little circles of black fondant for his pupils. Using a cotton swab, add just a tiny drop of water on one side and stick them onto the white circles **11**. Fasten the eyes to the cake with the cotton swab and water **12**. Next, shape a piece of black fondant into a thick circle about the same size as the eyes. Using the handle end of a wooden spoon, make two indentations for his nostrils **13**. (We used the end of a pen for this step.) Stick the nose about halfway up the side of the cake with the cotton swab and water.

THE HOOVES & TAIL: Make bison hooves from 2 fat circles of black fondant, each about the size of a silver dollar. Cut off the bottom third of each circle. Fasten the hooves at the bottom of the cake. Using the back of a knife blade, make a straight indentation in the middle of each hoof **14**. To make a tail, roll a thin snake of light brown fondant **15**, cut it to 3 inches or so, and fasten it right above where his butt would be on the back of the cake **16**. Take a tiny piece of dark brown fondant and make a little tuft of fur for the tip of his tail **17**. Fasten it to the cake with a tiny drop of water.

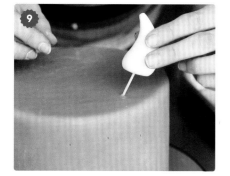  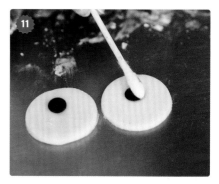

 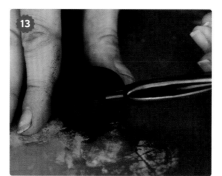 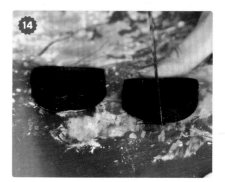

 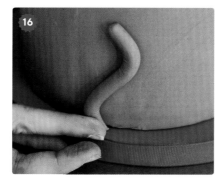 

THE HAIR: Using the dark brown fondant, make the bison beard and hair from blueberry-size pieces. Roll them into little chunks of hair and fasten them to the cake with a little water . You can also wet a small section of the cake and stick the hair to the wet spots. Now your bison is ready to roam!

CANDY MOSAIC CAKE

My mom is an artist. She's where I get my creativity from. She makes the most amazing mosaics and she always has fun making them, so I thought it would be fun to make a mosaic cake just like she does. The trick with this cake is to get good-looking candy. Go to a candy shop or look online and pick out candies with cool colors and different sizes. Another way to design this cake is to sketch it out first and then find candies that fit your sketch.

You can see the big cake on the next page doesn't match the cake we were making in the step by step on the next pages. That's because there's no one perfect way to make a Candy Mosaic Cake! Just let your imagination and creativity go wild and make you own amazing candy design!

THE CAKES: Bake any size and flavor cake you want. I'd start with 3 layers of a 6- or 8-inch round cake.

ICING & FONDANT: Ice the cake according to the instructions on page 20. Cover the cake with fondant according to the instructions on page 126. The fondant doesn't have to be perfect because you are going to cover the entire thing in candy. So, if there are creases or wrinkles in the fondant, it's totally cool. Just make sure you cover it completely.

DECORATE YOUR CAKE: Put your cake on a cake board. Cut a circle out of a flat piece of cardboard or, for a better-looking cake, a ¼-inch-thick piece of foam core cut to the size of your cake. If you use foam core, you can also get

a ¼-inch ribbon and run it around the edge. This will make your cake look more finished.

Make some royal icing from the recipe on page 21. Put like 4 tablespoons of royal icing in a piping bag and twist-tie the back of the bag so no air can get in. Store the royal icing in a bowl with a damp paper towel placed directly onto the royal icing.

Set up a decorating station. Put all your different candies into separate bowls so they are easily accessible. Keep some plastic piping bags handy in case you need a refill of icing. Put your cake onto a cake turntable or an upside-down plate so you can spin it easily. Put on some good music.

Optional! If you want, you can get a cool effect by carefully–super carefully!–holding the cake upside down and gently touching the royal icing to a plate of sparkles or sprinkles **1** **2**.

Cut a tiny hole in the pointy end of your piping bag. (If you want to place candy on the side of the cake, put a small dot of icing on to the back of it. That'll help it stay in place!) Place the candy where you want it to stick to your cake, and then wiggle it back and forth, so you spread the royal icing out underneath the piece of candy **3** **4** **5** **6**. Try a few variations and you'll find what works for you. This is a long process. Take your time and remember that nothing is permanent. If you don't like the direction your cake is going, just pop the candies off and start over.

To finish your cake, keep adding candies until the whole surface is covered. I also like to decorate the board that the cake is sitting on. Have fun!

Duff's Tip

Too much royal icing and the candy will slide down. Too little and the candy won't stick.

CARVED HEART CAKE

Nothing shows somebody that you love them quite like making them a cake. But what if the cake is a carved 3-D heart? I mean, I don't think there is any stronger way you could tell you someone you love them. Maybe make it a chocolate cake. That would make it special. Once you master carving the heart cake, you can then use those skills to carve literally anything. A skull, a football, a flower, a pile of mashed potatoes, a small badger, the number 4, an apple...

THE CAKES: Bake a 3-layer cake. Fill the cake however you want, but don't ice it yet—you're gonna carve it up. I would avoid complicated fillings. Use something simple. When you carve a cake with all kinds of crunchy stuff or sticky stuff inside the cake, it sticks to your knife and makes a big mess. Better to make a simple, delicious cake and enjoy the carving process instead of going crazy with honey and chopped peanuts stuck everywhere, tearing up your cake. The other option is to carve your cake one layer at a time—there's no right way—but just think it through before you start.

CARVING A HEART SHAPE: Put the stacked cake on a piece of cardboard. Get a big, empty bowl for all the cake you are going to carve away. Use this cake to patch any holes you accidentally make—and for snacking. (You can also use it to make cake-in-a-jar or cake pops.) Using a regular steak knife, carefully draw a heart shape into the top of the cake. Make the heart as big as the cake will allow. If you want, you can also draw a heart on piece of paper, cut the heart out with scissors, and use it to trace a heart onto the cake **1** if you don't feel comfortable free-handing it.

Now you should have a cake that is heart-shaped, flat on top, with sharp corners connecting the top and the sides. Here's the fun part. Using your knife, carve away at the corners at a 45-degree angle. A little at a time **2 3**. Go all the way around the cake. Now, did you carve enough? Look at it. I bet you didn't. Carve some more of the corner away. Remember, you want to make the heart have rounded edges. Like a big mylar balloon. Keep carving, stopping now and then to look at what you are doing. See where you need to carve more, and where you need to stop. You can see the cake in your mind; just make what you see in your brain happen on the cake.

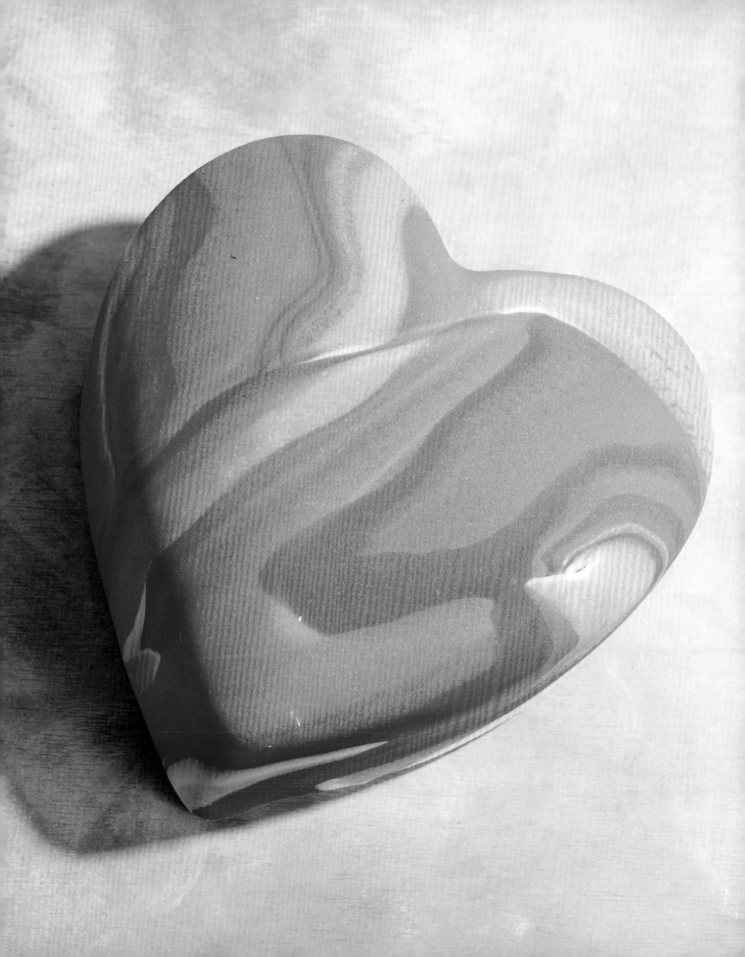

ICING THE CAKE: Now you should have a cake that is shaped like a heart. Ice the whole thing in buttercream with a small offset metal spatula **4** **5**. Or a butter knife if you don't have a spatula. If there are spots where you may have dug out a little too much cake, fill those spots in with cake or buttercream **6**. Fondant won't hide the imperfections. Once the cake is iced and nice and smooth, place it in the fridge for at least 1 hour so it sets up and gets firm **7**.

FINISHING YOUR CAKE:
Now you can decide whether to finish your cake in buttercream or fondant. If you are going to finish the cake in buttercream, make a red, pink, or honestly whatever color buttercream you want and ice the cake on a piece of cardboard. Place the cake in the freezer for about 30 minutes when you're done so you can transfer the cake to a nice cake board. You can put the cake on a round cake board or cut out a heart from a piece of ¼-inch foam core and put your cake on that. If you want to finish the cake in fondant, dye some fondant by kneading in the gel food coloring of your choice until the fondant is the color you want **8**. You can do a solid color, or, if you're feeling feisty, you can marble it **9** **10** **11** **12**. Cover the fondant with plastic wrap and let it rest for a few minutes while you trim the cardboard that the cake is sitting on. Roll the fondant out into a circle about ¼ inch thick **13** and drape it over the cake **14**. Gently smooth the fondant with your fingers **15** and then trim the bottom about ¼ inch above the table to allow the cake to settle a

bit **16** **17** **18**. If you are planning on airbrushing the cake, color the fondant in a light version of the color you want to airbrush. This makes it so you don't have to use a super-heavy coat of airbrush color and get the cake too wet.

Now your cake should be on a cake board and looking like a heart. Either it's finished OR you could keep going. Maybe add some

candy hearts to it with a little royal icing. Maybe write someone's name on it. If the cake is finished with buttercream, I would recommend writing the name in a different color buttercream. If the cake is topped with fondant, I would either write the name in royal icing or cut out letters in a different color fondant and place them on the cake with a little bit of water.

  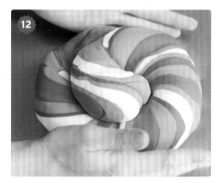

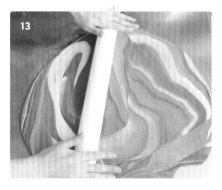  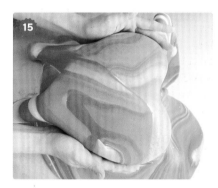

 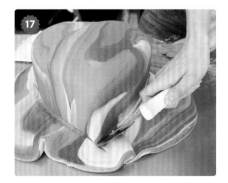 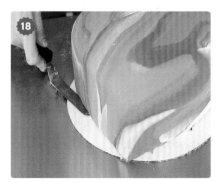

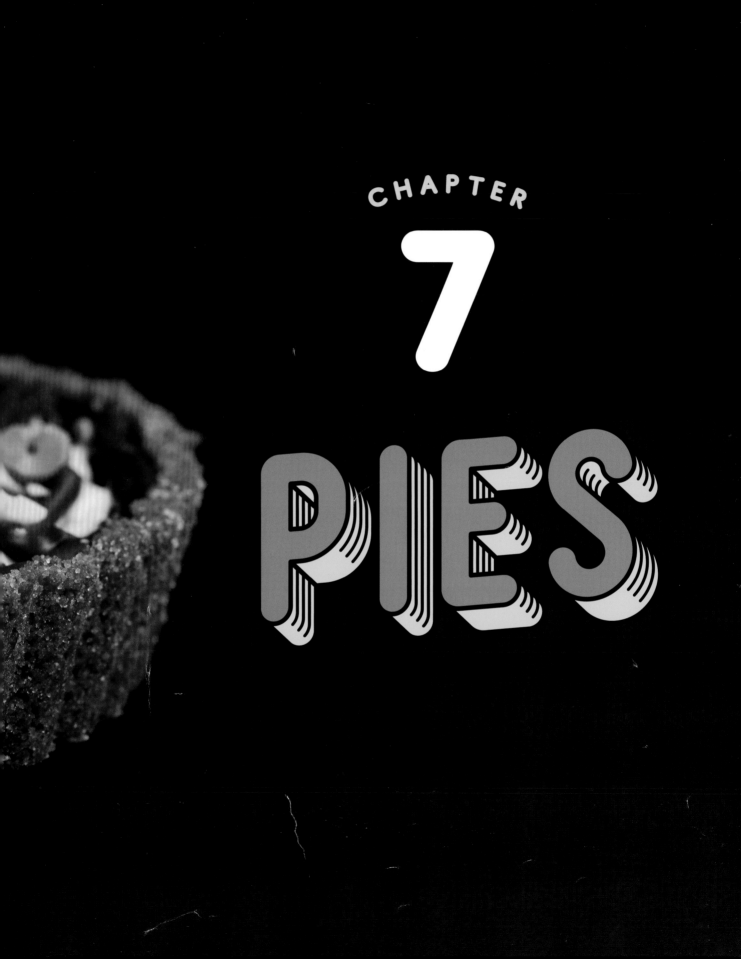

CHAPTER

7

PIES

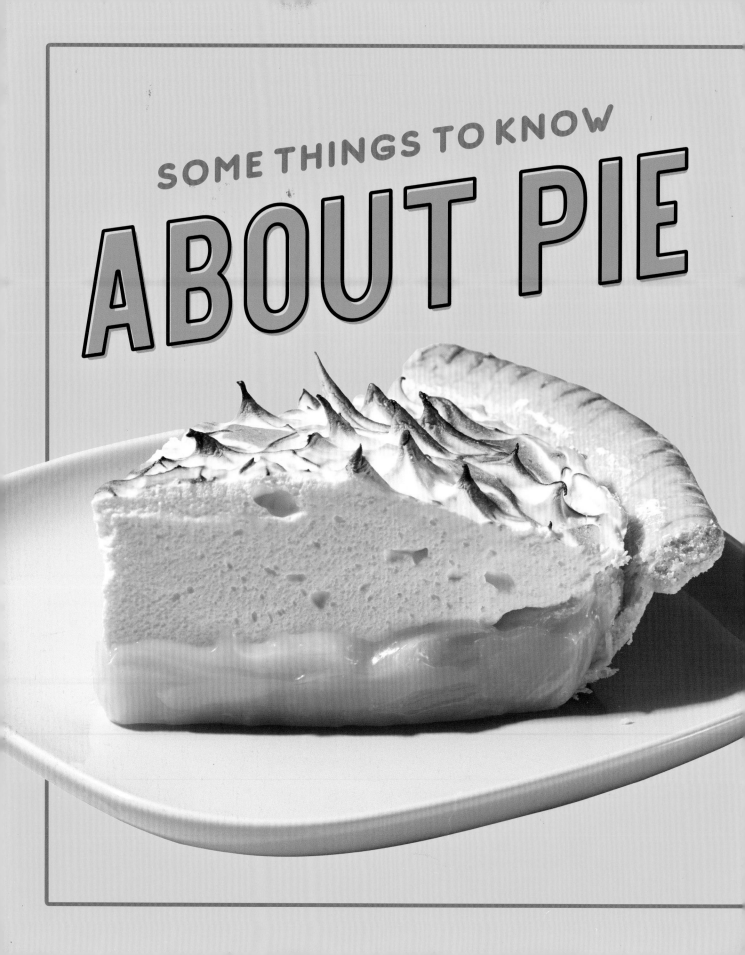

SOME THINGS TO KNOW
ABOUT PIE

Pies are not as hard as you think. Just like with anything in life, making a good pie consists of doing lots of little things correctly. Just be mindful and do each step in the process the right way, and you'll make awesome pies.

1 PIE DOUGH IS BASICALLY FLOUR, WATER, AND FAT.

Having good-quality flour and water are important, but the fat you choose is what really gives your pie its personality. Butter has the best flavor for pie dough, but it also has the lowest melting point, which can make the dough soft if it gets too warm. If you make an all-butter pie dough, it's super important to keep it cold. Lard makes the crispiest crust and has a really decadent texture, but it can taste a little like bacon (which is never a problem in my book). Vegetable shortening makes the crust keep its shape really well because it has the highest melting point, but it adds absolutely zero flavor. Some pie dough recipes use a combination of two or even three of the different fats for the best results.

2 WHEN TALKING ABOUT PIE DOUGH, YOU'LL HEAR THE WORDS TENDER, FLAKY, AND MEALY.

This is describing the crust after it bakes. Choosing the right fat will help you get the texture you want, but so will the liquid. Most recipes call for cold water, and those recipes are good. But to really get the crust you want, using the right liquids will make all the difference. Some recipes call for vinegar. The acid in the vinegar will make your crust much less tough

because it keeps the gluten from forming. Also, when you use vinegar, it helps to keep the pie crust from shrinking too much. Or, if you like the crust a little darker and richer, you can use milk. Milk will caramelize faster in the oven and adds richness and sweetness to the dough.

3 THERE ARE DIFFERENT TECHNIQUES FOR PIE TOPPINGS.

There are open-top pies with decorative edges. Some pies have a top crust or a latticed top. Some are topped with streusel. Working with pie crust doesn't have to be difficult; and once you have a recipe you like, the most important thing to remember is to keep the dough chilled while you are working with it. Work quickly—if the dough is too warm, it won't keep its shape. Also, the fat will melt into the dough and not be flaky. I like to put my pies in the freezer for 15 to 20 minutes before I bake them, so they really hold their shape in the oven.

4 I LIKE TO BAKE MY PIES ON THE BOTTOM RUNG OF THE OVEN.

My biggest pie fear is that the pie will bake and look good, but the bottom will still be soggy. Usually, the bottom rung is closest to the heat, so the bottom of the pie gets blasted and hopefully bakes all the way through. That's about it, so go to the farmers' market, get some beautiful fruit, and go bake a pie.

CHOCOLATE CREAM PIE

MAKES
1
9-inch pie

I don't think that there are three words in the English language that, when put together, sound more delicious than chocolate cream pie. As soon as you hear the words chocolate cream pie, you can already taste the chilled whipped cream, the smooth chocolate filling, and the crispy, crunchy crust. One of the things that makes food so delicious is anticipation. And I think the words chocolate cream pie trigger that anticipation.

PREP TIME
45 minutes

Ingredients

FOR THE CRUST
25 Oreo cookies

6 tablespoons (85 grams) unsalted butter, melted

Pinch of kosher salt

FOR THE GANACHE
8 ounces (227 grams) semisweet chocolate chips

8 ounces (227 grams) heavy cream

FOR THE CHOCOLATE WHIPPED CREAM

4 ounces (113 grams) cream cheese, at room temperature

⅓ cup (40 grams) powdered sugar

2 tablespoons (12 grams) cocoa powder

1 cup (225 grams) heavy cream

One 3.4-ounce box (96 grams) instant chocolate pudding

1 cup (240 grams) whole milk

FOR THE FILLING
4 ounces (112 grams) bittersweet chocolate chips

8 ounces (226 grams) cream cheese

¼ cup (50 grams) granulated sugar

FOR THE GARNISH
10 Oreo cookies, roughly chopped

Shaved white chocolate

Shaved milk chocolate

Shaved dark chocolate

Chocolate sprinkles

One 6½-ounce can whipped cream topping

EQUIPMENT

- **Food processor**
- **3 medium bowls**
- **Fork**
- **9-inch pie pan**
- **Small saucepan**
- **Whisk**
- **Rubber spatula**
- **Stand mixer**
- **Offset metal spatula**
- **Vegetable peeler**

RECIPE CONTINUES

MAKE THE CRUST

1 In the bowl of a food processor with a blade attachment, pulse the cookies until you get cookie crumbs.

2 Put the crumbs in a medium bowl, add the melted butter and toss with a fork to combine.

3 Press the cookies into pie pan and refrigerate for 30 minutes, or until you're ready to use it, whichever comes second.

MAKE THE GANACHE

4 Put the chocolate chips in a medium bowl and set aside.

5 Pour the cream into a small saucepan and, over medium-high heat, bring the cream to a boil.

6 Turn off the heat and pour the cream over the chocolate. Cover the bowl with a kitchen towel and let it sit for 3 minutes.

7 Remove the towel and whisk the ganache until it's shiny.

8 Pour half of the ganache into the pie crust and spread evenly all the way up the sides.

9 Pour the rest of the ganache into a piping bag and set aside at room temperature.

MAKE THE CHOCOLATE WHIPPED CREAM

10 In a medium bowl using a rubber spatula, blend the cream cheese, powdered sugar, and cocoa powder together until the mixture is light and fluffy.

11 Add the heavy cream and whisk until medium-stiff peaks form. (Make sure it doesn't get too stiff.)

12 Place the whipped cream in the fridge until you're ready to use it.

13 In another medium bowl, whisk together the instant pudding and the milk until it thickens.

14 Using a rubber spatula, fold half of the whipped cream into the bowl of pudding. Return both bowls of creamy pudding and remaining whipped cream to the fridge.

MAKE THE FILLING

15 In a microwave-safe bowl with the microwave on high, heat the chocolate chips in 10-second increments, stirring each time, until they're all melted.

16 Add the cream cheese and sugar and mix together.

FINISH THE PIE

17 Take the pie crust from the refrigerator. Using an offset metal spatula, spread the pie filling evenly into the pie crust.

18 Return the pie crust and filling to the fridge for 15 minutes to set.

19 Take the filled pie crust and the pudding-and-whipped-cream mixture from the fridge. Spread the mixture evenly over the pie filling. Refrigerate for another 8 to 10 minutes.

20 Remove the pie from the fridge and spread the remaining chocolate whipped cream over the pie.

21 Spray canned whipped topping all over the pie in a fun design.

22 Pipe the remaining ganache all over the pie.

23 Top with the chopped Oreos, shaved chocolate (shaved from a bar with a vegetable peeler), and chocolate sprinkles.

24 Wake up in 30 years from the deliciousness of your chocolate coma.

· DUTCH ·
APPLE PIE

My first job was at McDonald's, and I'd never had apple pie until I worked there. The McDonald's apple pie has a sweet, cinnamon crust stuffed with apple-flavored goo and chunks of apples. I think that McDonald's apple pie has been the pie with which I judge all other apple pies. Basically, this Dutch apple pie is my attempt at creating the McDonald's apple pie experience, except this one is actually shaped like a pie.

PREP TIME
1 hour
BAKING TIME
30 to 40 minutes

Ingredients

FOR THE CRUST

2 cups plus 3 tablespoons (325 grams) all-purpose flour, plus more for dusting

1 teaspoon (6 grams) kosher salt

1 tablespoon (13 grams) granulated sugar

1 cup (2 sticks or 230 grams) cold unsalted butter, diced into ½-inch cubes

1 tablespoon (15 grams) white vinegar

5 to 6 tablespoons (74 to 89 grams) ice water

1 large egg

Pinch of kosher salt

Pinch of granulated sugar

Few drops of water

FOR THE FILLING

3 cups (750 grams) unfiltered fresh apple cider

¼ cup plus 1 teaspoon (45 grams) cornstarch

¼ cup (50 grams) granulated sugar

2 teaspoons (8 grams) ground cinnamon

Pinch of ground nutmeg

Pinch of ground cloves

Pinch of ground allspice

Few drops of pure vanilla extract

8 tablespoons (1 stick or 113 grams) unsalted butter, cut into small cubes

6 or 7 medium apples (I like Fuji; use what you want)

2 tablespoons (25 grams) brown sugar

2 teaspoons (8 grams) ground cinnamon

Pinch of ground nutmeg

Pinch of ground cloves

Pinch of ground allspice

Pinch of kosher salt

FOR THE TOPPING

⅓ cup (67 grams) granulated sugar

¼ cup (50 grams) firmly packed light brown sugar

1 cup (150 grams) all-purpose flour

1 teaspoon (4 grams) ground cinnamon

Pinch of ground ginger

Pinch of kosher salt

½ cup (1 stick or 113 grams) cold unsalted butter

Coarse sugar, to finish

EQUIPMENT

- **4 medium bowls**
- **Whisk**
- **Paring knife**
- **Rubber spatula**
- **Plastic wrap**
- **Rolling pin**
- **9-inch pie pan**
- **Medium saucepan**
- **Paring knife**
- **Cutting board**
- **Large sauté pan**
- **Food processor**
- **Sheet pan**

RECIPE CONTINUES

MAKE THE CRUST

1 In a medium bowl, whisk together the flour, salt, and granulated sugar. Place the bowl in the fridge for 20 minutes.

2 Using a paring knife, dice the cold butter into ½-inch cubes and add to the mix. Toss so all the butter pieces get coated with flour. Rub the butter into the flour with your fingers.

3 Add the vinegar and water and toss with a rubber spatula gently until a dough forms. Try not to knead the dough, but if you have to, do it gently. You want the butter pieces to not be totally mixed into the dough.

4 Divide the dough into 2 disks, wrap in plastic wrap, and put in the fridge for 15 minutes.

5 Take 1 disk of dough out of the fridge and, using a rolling pin on a lightly floured surface, roll it out till it's at least 9 inches across and ⅛-inch thick, and then place into a pie pan.

6 Cut the dough about an inch wider than the pie pan. Fold the edges up and create a nice edge.

7 Refrigerate for 15 minutes.

MAKE THE FILLING

8 In a medium bowl, whisk together 1 cup of the cider and the cornstarch.

9 In a medium saucepan over medium-high heat, whisk the remaining 2 cups of the cider and the granulated sugar, salt, cinnamon, nutmeg, cloves, and allspice.

10 When the cider mixture boils, stir in the cornstarch mixture. When the goo gets thick and isn't cloudy anymore, pour into a clean medium bowl.

11 Add the vanilla and half of the butter cubes and stir to combine.

12 Cover the bowl and set aside.

13 Using a paring knife and cutting board, halve, core, and peel each apple and slice it into wedges.

14 In a large sauté pan over medium-high heat, melt the remaining butter.

15 Add the brown sugar, cinnamon, nutmeg, cloves, allspice, and salt to the melted butter.

16 When the brown sugar has melted and is bubbling, add the apples and sauté until the apples get caramelized and smell awesome.

17 Remove the pan from the heat and, using a rubber spatula, add the seasoned apples to the bowl of cider goo. Toss to coat.

18 Cover the bowl with plastic wrap and refrigerate for at least 45 minutes.

MAKE THE STREUSEL TOPPING

19 In the bowl of a food processor with a blade attachment, pulse the granulated sugar, brown sugar, flour, cinnamon, ginger, and salt and mix until it is incorporated.

20 Add the butter and pulse until the mixture is crumbly but not a paste.

21 Put the streusel in a medium bowl and refrigerate.

TO FINISH THE PIE

22 Put a rack on the middle rung of the oven and lay a sheet pan on the rack below it to catch any drips. Preheat the oven to 400°F.

23 Fill the pie crust with the filling.

24 Make an egg wash by whisking together the egg, salt, sugar, and water.

25 Using a rolling pin, roll out the other half of the pie dough and cut leaves out using a circle cutter.

26 Adhere the leaves to the edges of the pie crust with egg wash.

27 Brush the egg wash onto the edges of pie dough and the tops of the leaves. Sprinkle coarse sugar on top.

28 Refrigerate the pie for 10 minutes.

29 When the oven is ready, remove the pie from the refrigerator and generously cover the top of it with your streusel.

30 Bake for 30 to 40 minutes. The pie edges should be dark brown and crispy and the streusel should turn golden brown.

31 Let the pie cool for at least 1 hour before eating.

32 Serve with vanilla ice cream or a slice of melted cheddar cheese. Seriously, it's delicious!

Duff's Tip

I just learned that the difference between Dutch apple pie and regular apple pie is the streusel on top. If you don't like the streusel, you can put a top crust on this pie, but then it's no longer Dutch: You just call it apple pie.

GET TO KNOW YOUR STREUSEL

Streusel is the crumbly stuff on top of muffins and coffee cake. Basically, it is a mix of sugar, butter, and flour that is baked right on top of other baked goods. It adds texture and flavor and makes everything a little more interesting. Streusel can have nuts in it, or other kinds of grains like oats, or cinnamon, nutmeg, and other spices. Here are a few different streusel recipes that'll get you started, but streusel is very forgiving. Once you master the basics of streusel, come up with your own recipes and see what you can make with it. All these recipes have the same instructions. Mash everything up real good and then sprinkle it onto whatever you are baking before you put it in the oven.

BASIC STREUSEL

2 tablespoons (28 grams) cold unsalted butter

¼ cup (38 grams) all-purpose flour

2 tablespoons (23 grams) light brown sugar

Pinch of kosher salt

Pinch of ground cinnamon

OAT STREUSEL

¾ cup (113 grams) all-purpose flour

½ cup (45 grams) rolled oats

¾ cup (139 grams) lightly packed light brown sugar

Pinch of ground cinnamon

Pinch of ground allspice

Pinch of kosher salt

7 tablespoons (99 grams) unsalted butter

WALNUT STREUSEL

½ cup (93 grams) lightly packed light brown sugar

½ cup (65 grams) chopped walnuts

¼ cup (38 grams) all-purpose flour

¼ cup (½ stick or 57 grams) unsalted butter

Pinch of ground cinnamon

Pinch of ground nutmeg

Pinch of kosher salt

CHOCOLATE STREUSEL

½ cup (75 grams) all-purpose flour

3 tablespoons (38 grams) granulated sugar

1½ tablespoons (9 grams) cocoa powder

Pinch of kosher salt

5 tablespoons (71 grams) unsalted butter

2 ounces (57 grams) chocolate chips

PEANUT BUTTER PIE

MAKES

1

9-inch pie

Peanut butter is almost perfect, but sometimes I think it's a little too thick and sticky. When you take a bunch of whipped cream and fold it into the peanut butter, I think it makes a more perfect peanut butter. Maybe all peanut butter should be light and whipped and airy. I think my favorite thing about this pie is that it tastes like Reese's Peanut Butter Cups with a graham cracker crust.

PREP TIME
25 minutes plus 30 minutes for chilling

BAKING TIME
7 minutes (for crust)

Ingredients

FOR THE CRUST

7 tablespoons (100 grams) unsalted butter

1¼ cups (140 grams) graham cracker crumbs

½ cup (100 grams) granulated sugar

Pinch of kosher salt

½ teaspoon (2 grams) ground cinnamon

FOR THE GANACHE

8 ounces (227 grams) semisweet chocolate chips

8 ounces (227 grams) heavy cream

FOR THE FILLING

¾ cup (203 grams) creamy peanut butter (Skippy works well)

4 ounces (113 grams) cream cheese, at room temperature

1 cup (125 grams) powdered sugar

1 teaspoon (5 grams) pure vanilla extract

8-ounce tub (226 grams) frozen whipped topping, thawed

2 tablespoons (16 grams) crushed salted peanuts

EQUIPMENT

- Small saucepan
- Whisk
- 9-inch pie pan
- 2 medium bowls
- Kitchen towel
- Offset metal spatula
- Piping bag
- Stand mixer
- Rubber spatula
- Kitchen scissors

RECIPE CONTINUES ➡

MAKE THE CRUST

1 Preheat the oven to 375°F.

2 In a small saucepan over medium heat, melt the butter.

3 Whisk the graham cracker crumbs, sugar, salt, and cinnamon in a bowl.

4 Add the melted butter and mix well.

5 Press the crumb mixture into a pie pan and bake for 7 minutes.

6 Set aside the pan to cool.

MAKE THE GANACHE

7 Put the chocolate chips in a medium bowl and set aside.

8 Pour the cream into a small saucepan and, over medium-high heat, bring the cream to a boil.

9 Turn off the heat and pour the cream over the chocolate. Cover the bowl with a kitchen towel and let it sit for 3 minutes.

10 Remove the towel and whisk the ganache until it's shiny.

11 Pour half of the ganache into the pie shell and, using an offset metal spatula, spread evenly, all the way up the sides.

12 Put the shell in the fridge.

13 Put the rest of the ganache into a piping bag and set aside at room temperature.

MAKE THE FILLING

14 Into the bowl of a stand mixer with a paddle attachment, beat the peanut butter, cream cheese, powdered sugar, and vanilla until light and fluffy, about 5 minutes.

15 Using a rubber spatula, carefully fold in the whipped topping.

16 Remove the pie shell from the fridge and fill it with the peanut butter filling. Chill for 30 minutes.

17 Remove the pie from the fridge. Snip the pointy end of the piping bag with kitchen scissors, and then pipe a fun design with the chocolate ganache all over the pie.

18 Sprinkle the peanuts over the pie and chill until serving.

· LEMON ·
MERINGUE PIE

MAKES
1
9-inch pie

My friend Valerie Bertinelli loves lemons so much, I figured I'd better make a recipe just for her. When we're judging *Kids Baking Championship*, all the kids know that I love bacon and Valerie loves lemons. So, depending on who the kids are trying to impress, we either get desserts covered in bacon or desserts made with lemon. Good thing for me, I also really like lemon.

PREP TIME
1 hour
BAKING TIME
crust: 35 minutes
meringue: 20 minutes

Ingredients

FOR THE CRUST

2 cups plus 3 tablespoons (325 grams) all-purpose flour, plus more for dusting

1 teaspoon (6 grams) kosher salt

1 tablespoon (13 grams) granulated sugar

1 cup (2 sticks or 230 grams) cold unsalted butter, diced into ½-inch cubes

5 or 6 tablespoons (74 or 89 grams) ice water

1 tablespoon (15 grams) white vinegar

FOR THE FILLING

5 large (70 grams) egg yolks

6 tablespoons (60 grams) cornstarch

1⅓ cup (267 grams) granulated sugar

¼ teaspoon (2 grams) kosher salt

1½ cups (354 grams) water

½ cup (118 grams) lemon juice

2 teaspoons (10 grams) lemon zest

2 tablespoons (28 grams) unsalted butter

FOR THE MERINGUE

1 tablespoon (10 grams) cornstarch

⅓ cup (79 grams) cold water

1 cup plus 2 tablespoons (262 grams) granulated sugar

¼ teaspoon (1 gram) cream of tartar

5 large (175 grams) egg whites

½ teaspoon (3 grams) pure vanilla extract

Pinch of kosher salt

EQUIPMENT

- 2 medium bowls
- Whisk
- Paring knife
- Rubber spatula
- Plastic wrap
- Rolling pin
- 9-inch pie pan
- Parchment paper
- Dried beans
- Medium saucepan
- Small saucepan
- Stand mixer
- Offset metal spatula
- Wire rack

RECIPE CONTINUES

MAKE THE CRUST

1 In a medium bowl, whisk the flour, salt, and sugar. Place in the fridge for 20 minutes.

2 Using a paring knife, dice the cold butter into ½-inch cubes and add to the mix. Toss so all the butter pieces get coated with flour. Rub the butter into the flour with your fingers.

3 Add the water and vinegar and toss with a rubber spatula gently until a dough forms. Try not to knead the dough, but if you have to, do it gently. You want the butter pieces to not be totally mixed into the dough.

4 Press the dough into a flat disk, wrap it in plastic, and put it in the fridge.

5 Preheat the oven to 375°F.

6 Using a rolling pin on a lightly floured surface, roll out the dough to ¼ inch thick, and then drape it into a pie pan. Cut the dough about an inch wider than the pie pan. Fold the edges up and create a nice edge. Place the pie shell back in the fridge for 10 minutes.

7 Press some parchment paper or aluminum foil over the crust and then fill the crust with dried beans.

8 Bake for 20 minutes.

9 Remove the beans and parchment paper, poke some holes in the crust with a fork so you don't get bubbles, and then bake for another 15 minutes or until the crust is golden brown. Remove from the oven and set aside.

MAKE THE FILLING

10 In a medium bowl, whisk the egg yolks a little and set aside.

11 In a medium saucepan over medium heat, whisk the cornstarch, sugar, salt, and water until combined. Bring to a boil, whisking the entire time. Reduce the heat to medium-low, and then simmer for 1 to 2 minutes, or until the mixture begins to thicken.

12 Once the mixture has thickened, pour a spoonful of hot mixture into the egg yolks and whisk really good. Repeat with spoonfuls until about half of the mixture is in the egg yolks.

13 Pour the egg yolk mixture into the saucepan and bring to a boil over medium heat, whisking constantly. Cook for 3 minutes.

14 Remove the pan from the heat and whisk in the lemon juice, lemon zest, and butter. Set aside.

MAKE THE MERINGUE

15 In a small saucepan, whisk the cornstarch and water until the starch dissolves. Heat over medium heat until the liquid thickens and is less cloudy. Set aside.

16 In a medium bowl, stir together the sugar, salt, and cream of tartar with a teaspoon. Set aside.

17 In the bowl of the stand mixer with the whisk attachment on medium-low speed, whisk the egg whites and vanilla until the mixture gets frothy. Slowly add the sugar mixture, increasing the speed to medium until the eggs form soft peaks.

18 Add the cornstarch mixture a spoonful at a time, increase the speed to medium-high until stiff peaks form. Do not overmix.

TO FINISH THE PIE

19 Preheat the oven to 325°F.

20 Using a rubber spatula, pour the filling into the pie shell and, using an offset metal spatula, spread it evenly across the shell.

21 With an offset metal spatula, spread the meringue completely over the top of the pie, sealing in the filling. Use the back of a spoon or a spatula to make peaks with the meringue.

22 Bake for 20 minutes, until the meringue is golden brown.

23 Remove the pie from the oven, letting it cool completely on a wire rack at room temperature.

Duff's Tip

This pie is best eaten the same day.

CAN I KEEP MY EYES OPEN WHEN I'M BLIND BAKING?

Sometimes you want to bake a pie crust or other pastry before you fill it, because the filling doesn't get baked. For instance, if you put chocolate mousse in a hot oven it will become hot chocolate soup. So you have to bake the pie shell first. Basically, you make a pie dough (or whatever pastry you want), put it in the pie pan, and bake it all by itself. This is called blind baking. There are a few ways to bake the pie shell so that it keeps its shape while it's baking. One method is to put parchment into the shell and fill the shell with beans or rice to hold the shell down. You can use ceramic pie weights which are little clay balls, but dried beans or rice work just fine and are MUCH less expensive. Another method is to place another pie pan on top of the shell and bake it upside down.

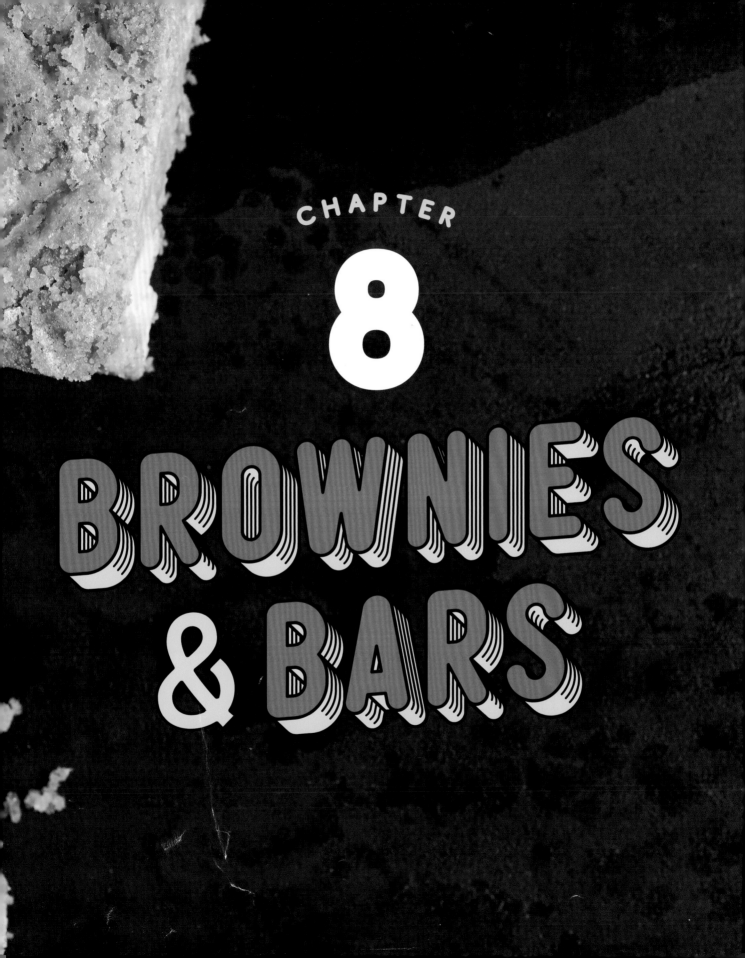

CHAPTER

8

BROWNIES & BARS

BLONDIES

Good blondies are like unicorns. There's a lot of blondies out there, but finding a really good one is rare. Blondies should be a little gooey and dense and buttery and rich. One thing they should definitely not be is cakey. This recipe uses brown butter. You can certainly bake these blondies with regular butter right out of the package, but the brown butter makes pretty good blondies into incredible blondies.

PREP TIME
20 minutes
BAKING TIME
35 to 40 minutes

Ingredients

1 ½ cups (3 sticks or 339 grams) unsalted butter

3 cups (600 grams) lightly packed light brown sugar

3 large eggs

1½ teaspoons (7 grams) pure vanilla extract

3 cups (450 grams) all-purpose flour

1 tablespoon (12 grams) baking powder

Pinch of kosher salt

¾ cup (130 grams) white chocolate chips (optional)

¾ cup (95 grams) chopped toasted walnuts (optional)

EQUIPMENT

- Medium saucepan
- Long-handled spoon
- Medium bowl
- Stand mixer
- Rubber spatula
- 9 × 13-inch baking pan
- Toothpick
- Chef's knife

 RECIPE CONTINUES

1 Preheat the oven to 350°F. Grease a 9 × 13-inch baking pan with cooking spray and set aside.

2 In a medium saucepan over medium heat, melt the butter and, using a long-handled spoon, scoop off all the foam. Continue to cook until the butter looks darker. There should be dark brown bits floating around, and it should smell exactly like heaven.

3 Transfer the browned butter to a medium bowl and let it cool in the fridge for 20 minutes, or until it starts to solidify.

4 In the bowl of a stand mixer with a paddle attachment, beat the cooled brown butter and brown sugar until the mixture is light brown and creamy. Using a rubber spatula, scrape the bowl.

Duff's Tip

Personally, I like wrapping the blondies individually, so I don't eat the whole batch in one go.

5 Add the eggs and vanilla and then mix well. Scrape the bowl.

6 Now add the flour, baking powder, and salt. Mix well on low speed. Scrape the bowl.

7 If you are adding white chocolate chips and/or nuts, do it now and mix very gently.

8 Using a rubber spatula, put the blondie batter in the baking pan and gently press down so it's even all the way across.

9 Bake for 35 minutes or until a toothpick inserted in the middle comes out mostly clean. (These blondies are best when they're slightly underbaked.)

10 Remove the pan from the oven, let the blondies cool completely in the pan, then remove them from the pan and, using a chef's knife, slice them into 12 bars.

WHAT IS BROWN BUTTER (AND WHY DO I LOVE IT SO MUCH)?

Butter is delicious and makes everything it touches better. But what if I told you there was an even better version of butter? Better butter? Impossible! Voilà—brown butter! Brown butter is butter cooked in a pan until all the water boils off and the milk solids and butter fat turn brown. Remember, browned things taste good. The flavor is rich and nutty and deep. It adds a level of flavor to things like cookies, cakes, and even sauces that you can't quite put your finger on but you know is good. It's also really easy to make. Chop 2 sticks of butter into small pieces and place in a skillet over medium-high heat. Melt the butter, stirring constantly. Soon, you will hear the butter pop and sizzle. Don't be alarmed; this is just the water leaving. Once the noise stops, keep stirring. You will start to see little brown flecks in the bottom of the skillet. This is good; those are the milk solids turning brown. Soon, you'll notice the liquid butter itself beginning to turn golden brown. Keep stirring and as soon as the butter is color you want it, dump it into a bowl so it stops cooking. Put the brown butter in the fridge and let it cool before using it.

FUN THINGS
TO PUT IN BLONDIES

My favorite blondies are made with toasted walnuts and white chocolate, but there are lots of other delicious things to put in blondies.

M&M's

Chocolate-covered malted milk balls

Peanut butter chips

Candied bacon

Toasted nuts, such as pecans or macadamias

Junior Mints

Yogurt chips

Coconut flakes

Brownie bits

Sprinkles

Oreo cookie crumbs

Caramel bits (salted or unsalted)

Nut brittle

Dried fruit, such as blueberries or cranberries

Toffee bits

Dates

Candied ginger

Maple sugar

Nougat

Chocolate-covered peanuts

White chocolate chunks

Peanut butter cups

Marshmallows

Butterscotch chips

· RAINBOW ·
UNICORN BROWNIES

MAKES
12
brownies

All brownies are magical. Brownies can literally make anyone smile. Even your principal – and she never smiles (especially not when you stuff a small piece of paper into the water fountain spigot and a laser beam of water shoots out and hits people in the face when they bend down for a drink. Not that I would know anything about that—wink, wink). But if all brownies are magical, the most magical brownies are rainbow unicorn brownies, with glitter. If you eat one after losing a tooth your tooth will grow back in 24 hours. They fix broken bones. They finish your homework for you. They are as magical as they are delicious.

PREP TIME
20 minutes
BAKING TIME
40 to 45 minutes

Ingredients

8 ounces (225 grams) white chocolate, chopped into little pieces

1 cup (2 sticks or 226 grams) unsalted butter, cut into little pieces

1½ cups (300 grams) granulated sugar

½ teaspoon (3 grams) kosher salt

1 teaspoon (5 grams) pure vanilla extract

2 large eggs

2¼ cups (282 grams) all-purpose flour

3 to 5 different gel food colors (whatever you want, to color the batter)

FOR DECORATING

3½ ounces (100 grams) white chocolate chips, melted, for drizzling

Edible glitter

EQUIPMENT

- 9-inch square baking pan
- Parchment paper
- Large microwave-safe bowl
- Rubber spatula
- 3 to 5 small bowls
- 3 to 5 piping bags
- Toothpick

RECIPE CONTINUES

1 Preheat oven to 350°F. Line a 9-inch square pan with parchment paper and set aside.

2 In a large microwave-safe bowl, melt the white chocolate and butter in 15-second increments (stirring with a rubber spatula between each increment).

3 Stir in sugar and salt and vanilla until well combined.

4 Add eggs and stir well.

5 Gradually add the flour to the batter, stirring until completely combined.

6 Separate the batter into 3, 4, or 5 bowls, depending on how many colors you want to make.

7 Stir a few drops of color into each bowl until you have the colors you want.

8 Using a rubber spatula, transfer each batter color to its own piping bag.

9 Cut the tip off of each bag and then pipe the colors into the baking pan. You can pipe in straight lines, squiggles, whatever you want, just remember that you are going to cut the brownies up, so make sure that every brownie gets all the colors!

10 Bake for 40 to 45 minutes (or until a toothpick inserted in the center comes out clean).

11 Allow the brownies to cool in the pan, then cut them into squares and drizzle top with melted white chocolate and edible glitter.

12 Allow the bars to set until the chocolate hardens and the magic works.

Duff's Tip

If you don't let the brownies sit for at least 10 minutes, you'll make a baby unicorn cry.

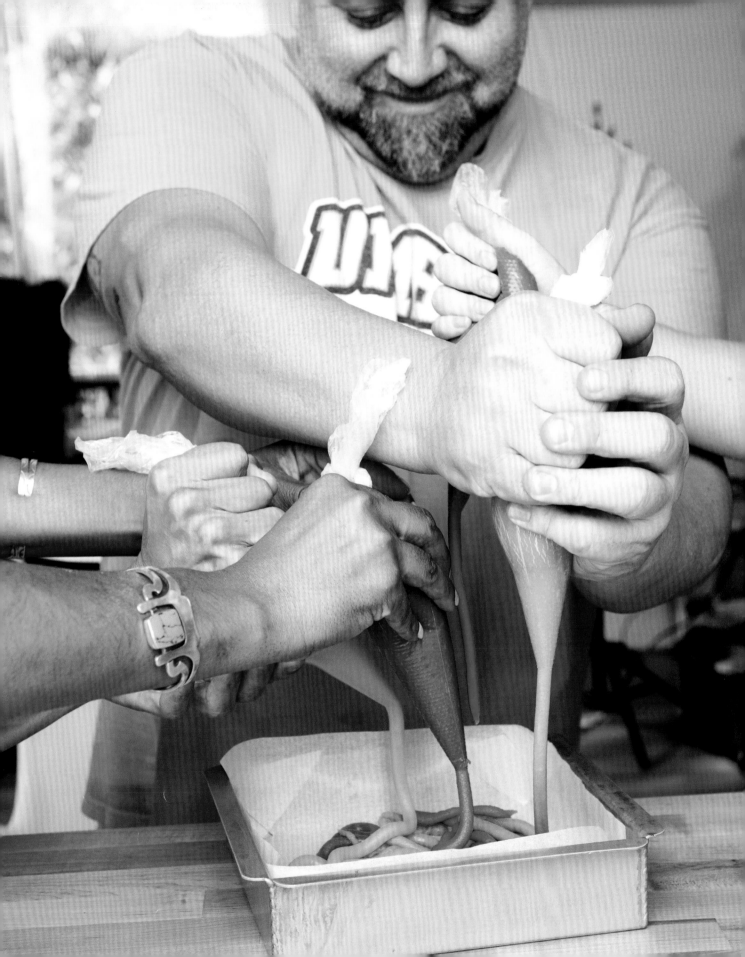

A LITTLE BIT ABOUT

COLOR

THEORY

Color theory is a set of ideas that help describe colors and their relationship to each other and to us. It is the science and art of using color. It helps to explain why certain colors look good together and how color is organized, so we can make sense of what we see.

First, colors are divided into two main groups. Primary colors are foundation colors, or those that cannot be made by mixing other colors. Primary colors include red, yellow, and blue. Secondary colors are colors that are made by mixing two primary colors together. Red plus blue makes purple. Red plus yellow makes orange (my favorite color), and yellow plus blue makes green. Purple, orange, and green are secondary colors.

All these colors can be arranged in a wheel so you can see their relationship to each other. As you look at the color wheel, draw a line from one color directly across to its color opposite. These are called complementary colors. Complementary colors are the most different from each other. They can really make things exciting, but too much and your eye can literally become tired from looking at them. Analogous colors are colors that are right next to each other on the color wheel. These colors are much more subtle and can be really pleasing to the eye. The third group of colors are called triadic colors. These can be found evenly spaced around the color wheel. Triadic colors are usually very bright and eye catching. Colors can also be divided into warm colors and cool colors. Warm colors are red, yellow, orange, and brown. Cool colors are blue, green, purple, and gray.

There are also ways to describe different kinds of color. This is called a hue. Hues are how we describe how much black, white, or gray has been added to a color. When you call a color a shade, you are describing how much black has been added, or how dark it is. When you call a color a tint, you are describing how much white has been added, or how light it is. When a color is called a tone, you describe how much gray has been added, or how muted it is. There are literally infinite kinds of color out there that can all be made with red, yellow, blue, black, and white.

Whenever we create anything artistic, no matter if it is food, or a picture, or some music, one of the things that makes us happy is finding the harmony in what we're making. You may have noticed that I put salt in almost every recipe in this book. That might seem weird, because everything in this book is sweet. But I'm trying to create harmony. Sugar, by itself, is sweet. You can add flour and butter and chocolate and all kinds of stuff and create different foods, but if you don't add any salt, there's a lack of harmony in how it tastes. You could say it tastes out of balance, or something is missing. The same thing happens in music. Play a note on a piano. Now play another note along with the first note. Some notes sound good together. Some don't. Finding the right notes that sound good together creates musical harmony. It's the same with colors. The right colors, whether they are analogous or complementary, create a visual harmony.

Here's the important thing: These are ideas based on mathematics, but never discount your eye, or your ear, or your tongue. You are the chef. You are the artist. You are the musician. You create the art and decide if what you made sounds good, looks good, or tastes good to you. Sometimes people won't taste or see the harmony that you see. That's okay. You decide what your own harmony is.

CHAPTER

9

TARTS

FRESH FRUIT
TARTS

MAKES

1

9-inch tart, or four 4-inch tartlets

This recipe is for one big tart, but if you want to get small, individual tart shells and make a bunch of little tarts, go right ahead. The shells of individual tarts will bake a little faster, so watch them carefully as they bake. Also, use any fruit you want. Apples and bananas don't work well because they get brown and mushy. You can also use just one kind of fruit or many different kinds. For this recipe, I used some figs from my tree in my backyard! Go foraging in your neighborhood and see what you can find.

PREP TIME
1 hour
BAKING TIME
15 to 18 minutes

Ingredients

FOR THE CRUST

3 large (42 grams) egg yolks

¼ cup (57 grams) heavy cream

2¾ cups (413 grams) all-purpose flour, plus more for dusting

1 cup (226 grams) cold unsalted butter, cubed

½ cup (100 grams) granulated sugar

Pinch of kosher salt

FOR THE PASTRY CREAM

4 large (56 grams) egg yolks

½ cup (100 grams) granulated sugar

3 tablespoons (30 grams) cornstarch

2 cups (480 grams) whole milk

Pinch of kosher salt

2 tablespoons (28 grams) unsalted butter, at room temperature

2 teaspoons (5 grams) pure vanilla extract

FOR THE TOPPING

½ cup (165 grams) apricot jam

2 tablespoons water

½ pint strawberries

½ pint blueberries

½ pint raspberries

1 kiwi fruit

1 mango

15-ounce can (425 grams) Mandarin orange slices, drained

2 figs

EQUIPMENT

- 2 small bowls
- Whisk
- Food processor
- Plastic wrap
- Medium saucepan
- Medium bowl
- Rubber spatula
- Rolling pin
- 9-inch tart pan
- Paring knife
- Fork
- Parchment paper
- Dried beans
- Oven mitts
- Wire rack
- Pastry brush

RECIPE CONTINUES

MAKE THE DOUGH

1 In a small bowl, whisk together the egg yolks and heavy cream.

2 In the bowl of a food processor with a blade attachment, pulse the flour, butter, sugar, and salt. Slowly add the yolk mixture to the flour mixture. Blend to combine, but don't overwork the dough.

3 Remove the dough and, turning it out onto a lightly floured surface, knead it 4 or 5 times to incorporate.

4 Divide the dough in half, flatten both pieces with your hands, wrap them in plastic wrap, and refrigerate one piece for 20 minutes. (Freeze the other piece for another project, for up to 3 months.)

MAKE THE PASTRY CREAM

5 In a small bowl, whisk together the egg yolks and ¼ cup of the sugar, until the yolks are lighter in color. Add the cornstarch, whisk again, and set the bowl aside.

6 In a medium saucepan over medium heat, combine the milk, remaining sugar, and salt and cook until the mixture almost boils.

7 Put the bowl of yolk mixture on a damp towel. The towel will ensure the bowl doesn't slide around. With one hand, start whisking the egg yolks; with the other hand, slowly drizzle the hot milk into the bowl containing the yolk mixture. Keep whisking until all the milk is incorporated.

8 Pour the custard back into the pot and continue cooking on medium-high heat, until the mixture is thick and one bubble plops up on top.

9 Remove the custard from the heat and pour into a clean medium bowl. Don't scrape the pot if the bottom looks burned or like scrambled eggs.

10 Now, stir in the butter and vanilla. Keep stirring until the butter melts. Place a piece of plastic wrap over the bowl so it is touching the pastry cream, and then refrigerate for 1 hour.

TO BAKE THE TART SHELL

11 Preheat the oven to 400°F.

12 Using a rolling pin, roll out the dough on a floured surface until it is a circle at least 9 inches across and ½ inch thick.

13 Lay the dough onto the tart pan and then, using your fingers, gently press it down. Try not to tear the dough or make it too thin. Ideally, it should be an even thickness all the way across.

14 Using a sharp knife, carefully trim the edges so the dough is perfectly even with the top of the tart shell.

15 Using a fork, poke a bunch of holes in the bottom of the tart shell to keep bubbles from forming during baking.

16 Refrigerate the tart shell for 20 minutes.

17 Remove the pan from the fridge and lay a piece of parchment over the chilled dough. Fill the uncooked tart shell with dried beans.

18 Bake for 10 minutes, then, using oven mitts, remove the pan from the oven. Remove the dried beans and parchment.

19 Return the pan to the oven, continuing to bake until the crust is golden brown, about 5 to 8 more minutes.

20 Let the pan cool on a wire rack.

Duff's Tip

Don't discard the scraps: If you poke any holes in the dough or if it tears, just fix it with dough scraps.

MAKE THE GLAZE
AND FINISH THE TART

21 In a medium pot over medium heat, cook the apricot jam and water. Stir it with a fork as it cooks until the mixture is a thin, shiny liquid.

22 Take the pastry cream from the fridge and, in the bowl of a stand mixer with a paddle attachment on medium-high speed, beat the pastry cream to loosen it up.

23 Spread the pastry cream in a thin ¼- to ½-inch layer on the bottom of the tart shell.

24 Carefully cut the strawberries, blueberries, raspberries, kiwi fruit, figs and mangos.

25 Arrange the fruit so there is no visible pastry cream. (You can make the tart look awesome by laying the fruit in cool patterns.)

26 Once the fruit is arranged, use a soft pastry brush to paint it with the warm apricot glaze. Don't leave any bare spots. Make sure to glaze all the fruit. Take your time.

27 Cut and serve immediately or refrigerate for up to 12 hours.

• PRETZEL-CRUSTED BUTTERSCOTCH •
BANANA CREAM TART

MAKES
1
9-inch tart

Butterscotch is caramel made with brown sugar. It's like caramel, but a little more interesting. Bananas are always great, but I think the star of this dish is the pretzel crust. It's crispy, buttery, and salty. It really goes well with the sweet vanilla pudding and butterscotch. Plus, it's really fun to say pretzel-crusted butterscotch banana cream.

PREP TIME
1 hour
BAKING TIME
12 minutes (for the crust)

Ingredients

FOR THE CRUST

2½ cups (110 grams) pretzels

½ cup (1 stick or 113 grams) unsalted butter, melted

¼ cup (76 grams) lightly packed light brown sugar

Pinch of kosher salt

FOR THE FILLING

1 cup (200 grams) granulated sugar

7 tablespoons plus 2 teaspoons (75 grams) cornstarch

½ teaspoon (3 grams) kosher salt

4 cups (960 grams) whole milk

2 tablespoons (28 grams) unsalted butter

2 teaspoons (10 grams) pure vanilla extract

2 ripe bananas, sliced into ½-inch-thick coins

Milk chocolate chips (optional)

FOR THE BUTTERSCOTCH SAUCE

1¼ cups (231 grams) lightly packed light brown sugar

Pinch of kosher salt

⅔ cup (215 grams) light corn syrup

¼ cup (57 grams) unsalted butter

1 cup (227 grams) heavy cream

2 teaspoons (10 grams) pure vanilla extract

FOR THE TOPPING

1 cup (226 grams) cream cheese, at room temperature

Pinch of kosher salt

¾ cup (94 grams) powdered sugar

A few drops of pure vanilla extract

1 cup (227 grams) heavy cream

Milk chocolate bar

EQUIPMENT

- Food processor
- Spoon
- 9-inch tart pan
- Wire rack
- 2 large bowls
- Whisk
- Medium saucepan
- Kitchen towel
- Rubber spatula
- Large saucepan
- Candy thermometer
- Wooden spoon
- Stand mixer
- Cheese grater, Microplane, or vegetable peeler

RECIPE CONTINUES

MAKE THE CRUST

1 Preheat the oven to 350°F.

2 In the bowl of a food processor fitted with a blade attachment, pulse the pretzels until they're finely ground but not turned to dust. Some pretzel pieces should still be intact. Add the melted butter and brown sugar to the crushed pretzels and pulse to combine.

3 Using a spoon, fill the tart pan with the pretzel mixture and shape it so the edges are crisp and it's about ¼ inch thick all over.

4 Bake for 12 minutes and cool in the pan on a wire rack.

MAKE THE FILLING

5 In a large bowl, whisk together the sugar, cornstarch, and salt.

6 In a medium saucepan over medium-low heat, warm the milk until it is above room temperature.

7 Put a kitchen towel under the bowl that contains the dry ingredients. The towel will ensure the bowl doesn't slide around. With one hand, start whisking the cornstarch mixture; with the other hand, slowly drizzle the hot milk into the bowl, whisking until all the milk is incorporated.

Duff's Tip

If you want to add milk chocolate chips to the bananas, go right ahead, Chef.

8 Pour the entire mixture back into the saucepan and cook on medium heat until the filling is thick. Don't let it boil.

9 Using a rubber spatula, pour the filling into a bowl, then stir in the butter and vanilla until the butter is melted and fully incorporated.

MAKE THE TART

10 Arrange half of the banana slices in the bottom of the tart shell.

11 Pour about half of the filling into the tart shell and spread it around evenly.

12 Eat the remaining pudding with a spoon. (It tastes better if you share.)

13 Arrange the rest of the bananas on the top of the pastry cream.

14 Put the tart shell in the fridge until you're ready to finish the tart.

MAKE THE BUTTERSCOTCH SAUCE

15 Clip a candy thermometer to a large saucepan. Add the brown sugar, salt, corn syrup, butter, and ¾ cup of the cream to the pan and heat over medium-high heat until it boils.

16 Turn the heat down to medium-low and slowly heat the sauce until it reaches 234°F. Don't stir it.

17 When the sauce reaches 234°F, take it off the heat and let it cool for 5 minutes. Slowly and carefully drizzle in the remaining cream and the vanilla while stirring constantly with a wooden spoon.

18 Pour the sauce into a large bowl, cover the bowl with plastic wrap, and set the bowl aside.

MAKE THE TOPPING

19 In the bowl of a stand mixer with the whisk attachment, whip the cream cheese, salt, powdered sugar, and vanilla until the mixture is light and fluffy.

20 Add the cream and whisk until stiff peaks form. Detach the bowl from the mixer and set aside.

TO FINISH THE TART

21 Remove the tart shell from the fridge.

22 Using a rubber spatula, generously cover the tart with the topping.

23 Artfully drizzle the butterscotch sauce over the pie.

24 Using a cheese grater, Microplane, or vegetable peeler, shave milk chocolate over the tart.

25 Slice and serve with more butterscotch sauce.

· NEW YORK ·
CHEESECAKE TART

MAKES

1

9-inch tart

When I was a kid, I had convinced myself that cheesecake was gross. Who would make a cake with cheese? I loved cheese. I loved cake. But cheese was for macaroni, not cake, right? Nobody told me it was cream cheese. Well, one day my mom's best friend came over and she said she had some cake for me. I was excited, as most kids would be, and I ate the "cake." It was sweet, creamy, and delicious. It had a graham cracker crust and cherry pie filling dumped all over it. I was hooked. I asked what kind of cake it was, and when I found out it was cheesecake, a whole new world of possibility opened before me. In this tart, the crust is baked, but the filling is not.

PREP TIME
35 minutes, plus 2 to 3 hours for chilling
BAKING TIME
10 minutes

Ingredients

FOR THE CRUST

1¼ cups (140 grams) graham cracker crumbs

½ cup (100 grams) granulated sugar

6 tablespoons (85 grams) unsalted butter, melted

Pinch of kosher salt

FOR THE FILLING

Two 8-ounce packages (452 grams) cream cheese, at room temperature

14-ounce can (397 grams) sweetened condensed milk

¼ cup (60 grams) fresh lemon juice

1 teaspoon (5 grams) pure vanilla extract

Pinch of kosher salt

FOR THE TOPPING

4 cups (about 2 pounds or 900 grams) pitted tart cherries

½ cup (120 grams) water

¼ cup (40 grams) cornstarch

¾ cup (150 grams) granulated sugar

Pinch of kosher salt

2 teaspoons (10 grams) almond extract

1 cup (236 grams) heavy cream (optional)

2 tablespoons (13 grams) sugar (optional)

EQUIPMENT

- **2 medium bowls**
- **Fork**
- **Cooking spray**
- **9-inch tart pan**
- **Stand mixer**
- **Metal offset spatula**
- **Medium saucepan**
- **Whisk**
- **Wooden spoon**

 RECIPE CONTINUES

MAKE THE CRUST

1 Preheat the oven to 350°F.

2 In a medium bowl using a fork, mix the graham cracker crumbs, sugar, melted butter, and salt.

3 Grease the tart pan with cooking spray.

4 Press the graham cracker crumbs into the tart pan until it looks flat and evenly pressed on the bottom.

5 Bake for 10 minutes.

6 Remove from the oven and let cool completely in the pan.

MAKE THE FILLING

7 In the bowl of a stand mixer with the paddle attachment on medium high speed, beat the soft cream cheese for 3 minutes.

8 Drizzle in the condensed milk a little at a time. Stop the mixer twice to scrape down the sides of the bowl and the beater with a rubber spatula.

9 Beat in the lemon juice, vanilla, and salt.

10 Pour the filling into the crust and smooth it out with a metal offset spatula.

11 Chill in the fridge for 2 to 3 hours.

MAKE THE TOPPING

12 Put the cherries and water in a medium saucepan, cover, and cook on medium-high until the cherries start to release their juice, about 4 minutes.

13 Reduce the heat to low and simmer, covered, for about 10 minutes. While the cherry filling is simmering, whisk the cornstarch, sugar, and salt in a bowl, until combined.

14 Uncover the saucepan and, using a wooden spoon, slowly add the dry mixture to the cherries, stirring constantly.

15 Remove the saucepan from the heat and transfer the cherry mixture to a medium bowl. Cover the bowl and refrigerate it for 20 minutes.

16 Remove the bowl from the fridge, add the almond extract, and then put the bowl back in the fridge until the filling is cold, about 20 minutes.

TO ASSEMBLE THE TART

17 Get fancy and make some whipped cream! Or not. You're the chef.

18 Take out your chilled cheesecake and cherry topping from the fridge.

19 Spread the topping in a nice, even layer on top of the cheesecake, add whipped cream if you made it, and then slice and enjoy.

20 Keep it refrigerated if you don't eat it all in one sitting!

CHOCOLATE CHEESECAKE

For a chocolate cheese-cake, follow the same instructions as above except add cocoa powder, melted chocolate, and use heavy cream in place of the condensed sweetened milk.

Two 8-ounce (397 grams) packages cream cheese, at room temperature

⅓ cup (65 grams) sugar

2 tablespoons (12 grams) cocoa powder

6 ounces (170 grams) semisweet chocolate, melted

¾ cup plus 1 tablespoon (185 grams) heavy cream

Pinch of kosher salt

1 teaspoon (5 grams) pure vanilla extract

Note

New York cheesecake is delicious. So are lots of other things in NYC. Turn the page for a list of my New York City favorites. →

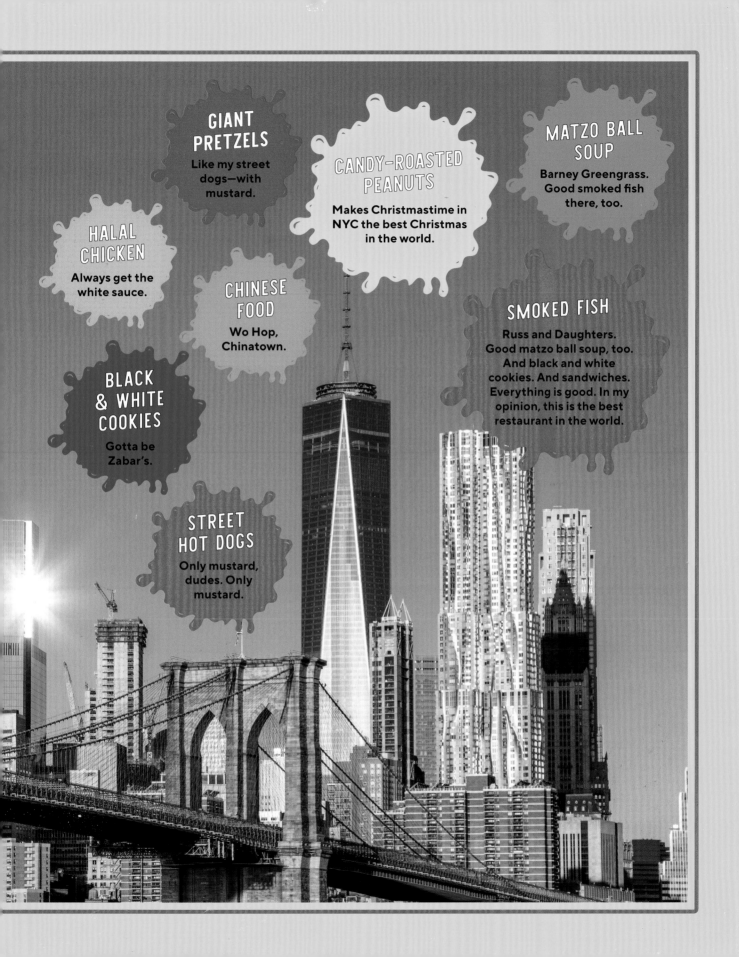

GIANT PRETZELS

Like my street dogs—with mustard.

CANDY-ROASTED PEANUTS

Makes Christmastime in NYC the best Christmas in the world.

MATZO BALL SOUP

Barney Greengrass. Good smoked fish there, too.

HALAL CHICKEN

Always get the white sauce.

CHINESE FOOD

Wo Hop, Chinatown.

SMOKED FISH

Russ and Daughters. Good matzo ball soup, too. And black and white cookies. And sandwiches. Everything is good. In my opinion, this is the best restaurant in the world.

BLACK & WHITE COOKIES

Gotta be Zabar's.

STREET HOT DOGS

Only mustard, dudes. Only mustard.

· GLOSSARY ·

BATCH an amount of baked goods made at one time

BATTER a semi-liquid combination of ingredients that is looser than dough

BEAT to mix ingredients together quickly, often with a whisk or mixer, which smooths and adds air into the mixture.

BLEND to mix together two ingredients until they don't separate

BOIL to heat a liquid to its boiling point, above 212 degrees, or adding an ingredient into a boiling liquid

BUTTERCREAM a fluffy frosting used to coat or decorate baked goods, which is made by creaming butter with powdered sugar and other ingredients

CARAMELIZE to heat sugar until it turns a golden brown

CHILL to cool food to less than room temperature

CHOP to cut food into small pieces

COAT to coat a food with another ingredient

COMBINE to mix two or more ingredients

CONSISTENCY a food's texture, such as thin or thick

COOL to allow a warm food to reduce in temperature

CREAM to mix ingredients into softened butter

CRUST the hard outer shell of a bread or pie

DISSOLVE to incorporate a solid ingredient into a liquid

DOUBLE BOIL to gradually melt an ingredient such as butter or chocolate over a pot of simmering water

DOUGH a combination of flour and a liquid that is thick enough to be kneaded or rolled

DRIZZLE to pour a thin stream of liquid over a food

DUST to sprinkle a thin layer of an ingredient over a food

EGG WASH a beaten egg mixture or brushing a beaten egg mixture over a food

FOLD to gently incorporate, often with a spatula, a light ingredient into a heavier ingredient

GARNISH to decorate a food

GLAZE to coat a food with a shiny layer of another ingredient, such as melted butter

GLUTEN proteins in grains that give food shape

GRAIN plant seeds from crops such as wheat

GRAINY describing the sandy texture of a food

GREASE to coat a pan with oil, cooking spray, or butter to stop food from sticking

INCORPORATE to completely mix one ingredient into another

KNEAD to press, push, and fold dough with the heels of your hands

LINE to cover the inside of a baking sheet with parchment paper or foil to stop food from sticking

MARBLE to partly mix two colors of batter or icing into a decorative swirl

MASH to smash or crush a food

MELT to heat a solid ingredient until it is a liquid

MISE EN PLACE a French phrase meaning "everything in its place," referring to having all of your ingredients and tools ready to use before starting to cook

MIX to combine two or more ingredients until blended

PINCH an amount of a dry ingredient, such as salt, that can be held between the thumb and forefinger

PIPE to squeeze a liquid though a piping bag for decorating

PREHEAT to heat an oven or pan to a specific temperature before putting food inside

PROOF to allow dough to rise before baking

PULSE to repeatedly turn on and off a blender/mixer to mix ingredients quickly but not fully

PUNCH to push down dough hard to expel gas and bubbles that have formed when dough rises

SAUTÉ to cook food in an uncovered pan using a small amount of fat

SCRAPE to use a flat or sharp tool to remove something from a surface

SIMMER to heat a liquid to a just below the boiling point

SOFT PEAKS to whip egg whites or cream until they slump over when you pull a spoon out

SPRINKLE to lightly scatter an ingredient over a food

SOFTEN to leave butter or margarine at room temperature until it can be easily spread

STIFF PEAKS to whip egg whites or cream until they stand up straight when you pull a spoon out

STIR to use a slow circular motion either to combine ingredients or to stop food from burning

TOSS to use two forks to mix lightly with a lifting motion

WHIP to stir a food using a fork, whisk, or mixer with short quick movements

WHISK to use a kitchen tool to beat and add air to a mixture

MEASUREMENT CONVERSIONS

EQUIVALENT MEASUREMENTS

1 tablespoon = 3 teaspoons = .5 ounce = 15 milliliter

¼ cup = 4 tablespoons = 2 ounces = 59 milliliters

⅓ cup = 5 tablespoons = 3 ounces = 79 milliliters

½ cup = 8 tablespoons = 4 ounces = 118 milliliters

⅔ cup = 11 tablespoons = 5 ounces = 158 milliliters

1 cup = 16 tablespoons = 8 ounces = 237 milliliters

1 pound = 16 ounces

½ pound = 8 ounces

BUTTER

½ stick = 4 tablespoons = ¼ cup

1 stick = 8 tablespoons = ½ cup

1 gallon = 4 quarts = 8 pints = 16 cups = 3.8 liters

1 quart = 2 pints = 4 cups = 950 milliliters

1 pint = 2 cups = 500 milliliters

EQUIVALENT TEMPERATURES

275° F	140° C	Very Cool
300° F	150° C	Cool
325° F	165° C	Warm
350° F	177° C	Moderate
375° F	190° C	Moderate
400° F	200° C	Moderately Hot
425° F	220° C	Hot
450° F	230° C	Hot
475° F	245° C	Hot
500° F	260° C	Very Hot

·INDEX·

A
airbrush, 125
American Buttercream
    for Confetti Cake, 133, 134
    for Cookies & Cream Cupcakes, 106, 108
    for Cupcake Christmas Tree, 116, 119
angel food cake, 125
Apple Pie, Dutch, 160, 161–163, *162–163*

B
baking pans, 11, *14, 15, 17,* 124
baking powder, 18, 79, 125–126
baking soda, 18, 79, 125–126
bamboo skewers, 13
Banana Cream Tart, Butterscotch, Pretzel-Crusted, *192,* 193–194, *195*
Bananas, Fried, 91, 92
Bark, Cookie, 35
Bear Claws, *76, 80,* 81–83, *82–83*
beignets, 70
bench scraper, *15*
Berliners, 71
Bertinelli, Valerie, 171
biscuit cake, 125
Bison Cake, 140, *141–143,* 142, 143
blind baking, 173
Blitz Puff Pastry, 44
Blondies
    Brown Butter, *174,* 175, 178, *179*
    fun things to put in, 179
Blueberry-Lemon Soup Dumplings, 93
borders, piping, 21, *21,* 126
Boston Cream
    Crepes, 93
    Donuts, Wicked-Good, 66, *67–69, 68–69*
Bread Pudding, Cake Donut, 62, *63, 64,* 65
Brown Butter, 178
    Blondies, *174,* 175, 178, *179*
brownies
    Cookie-Stuffed, 35
    Rainbow Unicorn, *180,* 181–182, *182–183*
    for Stuffed-Crust Dessert Pizza, 99, 100
Bundt Cake, Chocolate, *128,* 129–130, *131*
Bundt pan, *13*
Buñuelos, 70
Burritos, Peaches-and-Cream, 93
butter, 18
    brown, 178
    creaming sugar and, 11
    measurements for, 204
butter cake, 125

buttercream, 202
    for Clementine Cake, 136, 138
    for Cookies & Cream Cupcakes, 106, 108
    for Cupcake Christmas Tree, 116, 119
    types of, 124
    for Unicorn Cupcakes, 111, 112, *114*
buttermilk, 18
butterscotch
    Banana Cream Tart, Pretzel-Crusted, *192,* 193–194, *195*
    Sauce, 193, 194

C
Cake Donut Bread Pudding, 62, *63, 64,* 65
cake hoops, 79
cake pans, 124
cake ring, 124
cake rounds, 124
cakes, *122,* 123–151, *127. See also* Cupcakes
    basic information about, 124–126
    birthday, 79
    Bison, 140, *141–143,* 142, 143
    Candy Mosaic, 144, *145,* 146, *146, 147*
    Carved Heart, 148, *149–151,* 150
    Chocolate, made with crepes, 93
    Chocolate Bundt, *128,* 129–130, *131*
    Clementine, 136, *137–139,* 138–139
    Confetti, *132,* 133–135, *134–135*
    crumb-coating, 20, *20,* 124
    decorating, 126
    filling, 22, *22,* 126
    Icebox Cookie Cake, 35
    icing, 20, 124, 126
    science of, 125–126
    stacking, 22, *22,* 126
    types of, 125
cake saw, 124
cake stand, 125
cake tester, 124
cake turntable, 124
candies, 96–97
Candy Mosaic Cake, 144, *145,* 146, *146, 147*
candy thermometer, *14*
can opener, *14*
Carved Heart Cake, 148, *149–151,* 150
Charm City Cakes, 79
Cheesecake, Chocolate, 199
Cheesecake Tart, New York, *196,* 197–199, *198–199*
chef's knife, *14*
chiffon cake, 125
chocolate, 18
    Bundt Cake, *128,* 129–130, *131*
    Cake, made with crepes, 93
    Cheesecake, 199
    coating, 18
    Cream Pie, 156, *157–159,* 158–159
    Fudge, 94, *95*
    Glaze, for Boston Cream Donuts, 66, 69

    sixlets, *17*
    Streusel, 164
    Whipped Cream, 156, 158
Chocolate Chip Cookies, Classic, *28,* 29–30, *30*
chop, 202
Christmas Tree, Cupcake, 116, *117–120,* 119–120
churros, 57, *58,* 59, *59,* 70
Cinnamon Sauce, for Monkey Bread, 84, *85,* 86
citrus
    candied, 138
    zest, 19
Classic Chocolate Chip Cookies, *28,* 29–30, *30*
Clementine Cake, 136, *137–139,* 138–139
coating chocolate, 18
cocoa powder, 18
Coconut Macaroons, 91, 92
color theory, 184–185
Confetti Cake, *132,* 133–135, *134–135*
Confetti Snickerdoodles, 32, *33,* 34, *34*
consistency, 202
cookbooks, 79
Cookie Bark, 35
cookie cutters, *13*
Cookie Fudge, 35
Cookie Milkshake, 35
Cookie Pops, 35
Cookie Pudding Pops, 35
cookies, *26,* 27–41
    Classic Chocolate Chip, *28,* 29–30, *30*
    Confetti Snickerdoodles, 32, *33,* 34, *34*
    cookie sandwich fillings, 40
    ice-cream cookie sandwiches, 31
    Peanut Butter Cookie Sandwiches, 36, *37–39,* 38–39, *41*
    using store-bought cookies, 35
Cookies & Cream Cupcakes, 106, *107,* 108
Cookie-Stuffed Brownies, 35
Cookie Surprise, 35
cooking spray, 18
cooling foods, 10, 202
cooling rack, *12,* 124
cornets, 21, *21*
coulis, 22, *22*
cracking eggs, 9, *9*
cream, 202
Cream Cheese
    Cookie-Sandwich Filling, 40
    Filling, for Cookies & Cream Cupcakes, 106, 108
creaming butter and sugar, 11
cream of tartar, 125–126
Creamy White Cookie-Sandwich Filling, 40
Crepe Lasagna, 93
crepes, 91–93
crumb coat, 124, 126
crumb-coating cakes, 20, *20*
crust, 202

Cupcake Christmas Tree, 116, *117–120*, 119–120
cupcake liner, *15*
cupcake pan, *17*
cupcakes, *104*, 105–121
    Cookies & Cream, 106, *107*, 108
    Cupcake Christmas Tree, 116, *117–120*, 119–120
    eating, the Duff way, 109
    Unicorn, *110*, 111–114, *112–114*
custard, 65
    frozen, 75
cutting foods, 10, *10*

D

dangerous objects, 8
decorating cakes, 126
decorating techniques, 20–22, *20–22*
deep frying, 56
deli cup, *17*
Dessert Pizza, Stuffed-Crust, *98*, 99–102, *100–103*
Dessert Tacos, L.A. Street, *90*, 91–92
digital scale, *16*
Diplomat Cream, 51, 52, 54
doneness, testing, 10
Donut-Flavored Plastic Bag Ice Cream, *72*, 73–74, *74*
Donut(s), *60*, 61–74
    from around the world, 70–71
    Cake, Bread Pudding, *62*, *63*, *64*, 65
    Flavored Plastic Bag Ice Cream, *72*, 73–74, *74*
    Wicked-Good Boston Cream, 66, *67–69*, 68–69
double boiler, 11, *11*
dough, 202
Dumplings, Blueberry-Lemon, 93
dust, 20, *20*, 202
Dutch Apple Pie, *160*, 161–163, *162–163*
Dutch-process cocoa powder, 18

E

Éclairs, Rainbow, *50*, 51, 52, *53–55*, 55
eggs, 9, *9*, 18
egg wash, 202
electricity, water and, 8
Equipment. *See* Tools and equipment

F

filling cakes, 22, *22*, 126
fine mesh strainer, *15*
fires, 8
flour, 18, 79
flourless cake, 125
folding, 11, *11*, 202
fondant
    for Bison Cake, 140
    for Candy Mosaic Cake, 144
    for Carved Heart Cake, 150, *151*
    Marshmallow, for Unicorn Cupcakes, 112, *113*
    rolled, 124, 126
food coloring, 18–19

French buttercream, 124
Fresh Fruit Tart, 188, *189–191*, 190–191
Fried Bananas, 91, 92
frosting (icing), 124
    buttercream, 124 (*See also* Buttercream)
    for Candy Mosaic Cake, 144
    for Carved Heart Cake, 150, *150–151*
    for Confetti Cake, 133, 134
    for Cookies & Cream Cupcakes, 106, 108
    for Cupcake Christmas Tree, 116, 119
    royal icing, 21, 124
    for Unicorn Cupcakes, 111, 112, *114*
Fruit Tart, 188, *189–191*, 190–191
Fudge, 94, *95*
    Cookie, 35

G

ganache, 21
    for Chocolate Bundt Cake, 129, 130
    for Chocolate Cream Pie, 156, 158
    for Neapolitan Profiterole Sundae, 47, 48
    for Peanut Butter Cookie Sandwiches, 36, 38
    for Peanut Butter Pie, 166, 168
garnish, 202
glaze, 202
    for Boston Cream Donuts, 66, 69
    for Fresh Fruit Tarts, 191
    for Rainbow Éclairs, 51, 54
gluten, 89, 202
grain, 202
grater, *13*
gum paste, 124

H

Heart Cake, Carved, 148, *149–151*, 150
high-ratio cakes, 125
history of baking, 78–79
Hot Fudge Sauce, 47, 48
hot glue, 121
hot objects, 8

I

Icebox Cookie Cake, 35
ice cream
    cookie sandwiches, 31
    Plastic Bag, Donut-Flavored, *72*, 73–74, *74*
    science of, 75
icing cakes, 20, 124, 126, *126*. *See also* Frosting (icing)
incorporate, 202
ingredients, 18–19
    amounts of, 23
    bringing to room temperature, 10
    history of, 78–79
    measuring, 25
Italian buttercream, 124

K

Kids Baking Championship, 24, 109, 171
kitchen safety, 8
knead, 202
knives, 8, *14*
Krispy Kookie Treats, 35

L

L.A. Street Dessert Tacos, *90*, 91–92
ladle, *16*
Lasagna, Crepe, 93
leaveners, 78, 79, 89
leavening, 125–126
Lemon Meringue Pie, *170*, 171–173, *172–173*
lifting, 8
line, 202
loaf pan, *13*

M

Macaroons, Coconut, 91, 92
malasadas, 70
marble, 202
Marshmallow Cream Cookie-Sandwich Filling, 40
Marshmallow Fondant, for Unicorn Cupcakes, 112, *113*
marzipan, 19
math, 25
measurement, 25
measurement conversions, 204
measuring cups, *14*
measuring spoons, *12*
Meringue, for Lemon Meringue Pie, 171–173, *172*, *173*
metal spatula, *17*
metal tongs, *14*
milk, 19
mise en place, 6, 7–23, 202
    decorating techniques, 20–22, *20–22*
    ingredients, 18–19
    kitchen basics, 9–11
    kitchen safety, 8
    tools and equipment, 12–17
mixers, stand, 10, *15*
mixing bowls, *15*
molasses, 19
Monkey Bread, 84, *85–88*, 86–87
muffin scoop, *12*

N

natural cocoa powder, 18
Neapolitan Profiterole Sundae, 46, 47–48
New York Cheesecake Tart, *196*, 197–199, *198–199*
New York City foods, 200–201
notes, taking, 23, 25
nuts, 11, 19

O

Oat Streusel, 164
offset spatulas, *16*
oil, 19
    cooking spray, 18
    for deep-frying, 56

Oliebollen, 71
Oreo Crust, for Cookies & Cream
    Cupcakes, 106, 108
ovens, 8–10, 78, 79

P
paint brush, *14*
pans
    baking (*See* Baking pans)
    sauté, *16*
parchment paper, *17*
Pastillaria, 78
pastry brush, *14*
Pastry Cream, for Fresh Fruit Tarts, 188,
    190
pâte à choux, *42,* 43–59
    Blitz Puff Pastry, 44
    Churros, 57, *58,* 59, *59*
    Neapolitan Profiterole Sundae, *46,*
        47–48
    Pâte à Choux recipe, 45
    Rainbow Éclairs, *50,* 51, 52, *53–55,* 55
    science of, 49
Peaches-and-Cream Burritos, 93
Peanut Butter
    Cookie Sandwiches, 36, *37–39,* 38–39,
        41
    Cookie-Sandwich Filling, 40
    Pie, 166, *167–169,* 168
Phyllo "Slaw," 91, 92
pie dough, 155
pies, *152,* 153–173, *154*
    blind baking shells, 173
    Chocolate Cream, 156, *157–159,*
        158–159
    Dutch Apple, *160,* 161–163, *162–163*
    facts about, 155
    Lemon Meringue, *170,* 171–173, *172–173*
    Peanut Butter, 166, *167–169,* 168
    streusel, 164, *165*
    toppings for, 155
pinch, 203
pipe, 203
piping borders, 21, *21,* 126
piping tips, *12–13*
Pizza, Stuffed-Crust Dessert, *98,* 99–102,
    100–103
pizza cutter, *13*
Plastic Bag Ice Cream, Donut-Flavored,
    72, 73–74, *74*
plastic wrap, *17*
Pops, Cookie, 35
pound cake, 125
powdered sugar, dusting with, 20, *20*
preheating, 10, 203
Pretzel-Crusted Butterscotch Banana
    Cream Tart, *192,* 193–194, *195*
Profiteroles, Neapolitan Sundae, *46,*
    47–48
proof, 203
Pudding Pops, Cookie, 35
Puff Pastry, Blitz, 44

pulse, 203
punch, 203

R
Rainbow Buttercream, for Unicorn
    Cupcakes, 111, 112, *114*
Rainbow Éclairs, *50,* 51, 52, *53–55,* 55
Rainbow Unicorn Brownies, *180,* 181–182,
    182–183
ramekins, *17*
recipes, reading and taking notes on, 23,
    25
Red Velvet Sauce, for Stuffed-Crust
    Dessert Pizza, 99, 101–102
rolled fondant, 124, 126
rolling pin, *12*
royal icing, 21, 124
rubber spatula, *12*

S
safety, 8, 56, 121
salt, 19, 185
sanding sugar, 19
Sauce
    Butterscotch, 193, 194
    Cinnamon, 84, *85,* 86
    Hot Fudge, 47, 48
    Red Velvet, 99, 101–102
sauté, 203
sautéing, 11, *11*
sauté pan, *16*
scale, digital, *16*
science
    of cakes, 125–126
    color theory, 184–185
    of ice cream, 75
    of pâte à choux, 49
    of yeast, 89
scissors, *12*
scrape, 203
scrapers, *15*
separating eggs, 9, *9*
Sfenj, 71
simmer, 203
Snickerdoodles, Confetti, 32, *33,* 34, *34*
soften, 203
soft peaks, 203
spatulas, *12, 16, 17*
spices, 19, 79
sponge cake, 125
spoons, *17*
    measuring, *12*
    wooden, *17*
spreader, *13*
sprinkles, 19
squeeze bottle, *14*
stacking cakes, 22, *22,* 126
stand mixers, 10, *15*
stiff peaks, 203
strainer, *15*
Strawberry Whipped Cream, for
    Neapolitan Profiterole Sundae,
    47, 48

streusel, 22, *22,* 165
    for Dutch Apple Pie, 161, 163
    types of, 164
Stuffed-Crust Dessert Pizza, *98,* 99–102,
    100–103
sufganiyot, 71
Sugar, 19
    creaming butter and, 11
    powdered, dusting with, 20
    sanding, 19
Sundae, Neapolitan Profiterole, *46,* 47–48
Suzettes, 93
Swiss buttercream, 124

T
Tacos, L.A. Street Dessert, *90,* 91–92
Tarts, *186,* 187–190
    Fresh Fruit, 188, *189–191,* 190–191
    New York Cheesecake, *196,* 197–199,
        198–199
    Pretzel-Crusted Butterscotch Banana
        Cream, *192,* 193–194, *195*
temperatures
    equivalent, 204
    for ingredients, 10
toasting nuts, 11
tongs, *14*
tools and equipment, *12–17*
    for baking cakes, 124–125
    history of, 78, 79
    learning about, 9
    safety with, 8
    storing, 8
toss, 203
turntable, cake, 124

U
Unicorn Cupcakes, *110,* 111–114, *112–114*
unicorns, facts about, 115

V
vanilla, 19

W
Walnut Streusel, 164
washing knives, 8
wax paper, *17*
weighing ingredients, 25
whip, 203
whipped cream, 22
    chocolate, 156, 158
    strawberry, 47, 48
whipping cream, 22
whisk, 203
Wicked-Good Boston Cream Donuts, 66,
    67–69, 68–69
wire whisk, *13*
wooden spoon, *17*

Y
yeast, 78, 89
Youtiao, 71

Z
zest, 19

ACKNOWLEDGMENTS

Writing a book is HARD! I had lots of friends help me do it. When you have a really big project you want to do, it's always better when you have some friends. My friends **ALEX MARGUERITE** and **JOE LAZO** helped me bake all the good stuff in this book and my other friends **APRIL RANKIN** and **MICAH MORTON** made all the things we baked look nice so that my friend **EVI ABELER** could take pictures of it. My friends **ELLEN SCORDATO** and **RICK FARLEY** made sure we knew what to bake and when and also made sure that we were actually working and not just listening to music and goofing off. My friend **DAVID LINKER** made sure I spelled everything write. My real good friend **TARA MASCARA** made sure I looked nice so when Evi took pictures of me I didn't look like a goblin. My friend **LISA SHOTLAND** brought us all yummy stuff to eat while we were baking like bagels and soup and pizza because we couldn't just eat cake and pie all the time. My best friend in the whole world **JOHNNA** taste-tested all the things we baked and told us if they were good enough for you. And my really good friend **KAITLYN LEONARD** did everything. She baked lots of this stuff, and told me when to write things, and kept track of how much sugar to put in stuff, and generally just kept me focused because I have the attention span of a fish and if nobody told me what and when to do things I would probably be wandering around in the woods looking at squirrels and leaves and birds and stuff. But my biggest thank you is for **YOU**. You want to bake and that makes me happy because I want to bake, and because you want to bake you make me feel like I chose to do something with my life that people like. So thanks for that.

♡ DUFF